FOLLOWERSHIP

FOLLOWERSHIP

The Leadership Principle That
No One Is Talking About

TRACEY ARMSTRONG

DESTINY IMAGE® PUBLISHERS, INC.

P.O. Box 310, Shippensburg, PA 17257-0310

"Speaking to the Purposes of God for This Generation and for the Generations to Come."

This book and all other Destiny Image, Revival Press, MercyPlace, Fresh Bread, Destiny Image Fiction, and Treasure House books are available at Christian bookstores and distributors worldwide.

For a U.S. bookstore nearest you, call 1-800-722-6774.
For more information on foreign distributors, call 717-532-3040.
Reach us on the Internet: www.destinyimage.com.

Trade Paper ISBN 13: 978-0-7684-3225-1
Hardcover ISBN 13: 978-0-7684-3407-1
Large Print ISBN 13: 978-0-7684-3408-8
Ebook ISBN 13: 978-0-7684-9069-5

For Worldwide Distribution, Printed in the U.S.A.

1 2 3 4 5 6 7 8 9 10 11 / 13 12 11 10

ENDORSEMENTS

Tracey Armstrong is a leader. In his family, church, and community, he is making an impact. That's the kind of man that I can follow. He will help you get where you want to go in the fulfillment of your destiny. *Followership* brings insight that we all need. Tracey brings a revelation that will build teams, grow organizations, and bless churches. Read it, meditate on it, and put it to use; it works.

Casey Treat
Christian Faith Center

As someone personally influenced by Tracey's teachings and leadership, I find that in *Followership*, he reinforces the idea that in order for us to really be effective leaders, we must first be followers... servants. Tracey keys in on the fact that only one title will make you successful... "well done good and faithful *servant*." Tracey so pointedly reminds us as leaders that your followers will take on your characteristics, good or bad,... and reveals the truths about developing and replicating through great leadership—great followers! Every leader as well as every person called to serve (all of us) should read this insightful book.

Joel Luce, CEO
ABG Marketing and Business Communications

It's been a joy of mine to see Tracey's journey, beginning with his young adult years, as he has developed into an outstanding person and great leader. His gifting and insight will challenge and sharpen you as you reach for the next level in your life and leadership.

Kevin Gerald
Champion Centre
Tacoma, Washington

The motivation, desire, and enthusiasm necessary to sustain change and growth within an organization requires a healthy relationship and balance between the leader and those being led.

While the material on leadership today is indeed prolific, the available information on those who are intended to follow leaders is minimal by comparison. Tracey Armstrong is a fresh, vibrant voice in contemporary culture. He is an emerging leader with a great capacity for influencing change and growth in his own sphere as well as within the sphere of other leaders who look to him for cues to effective sustainability of the vision with which they have been entrusted.

Tracey's work in *Followership* provides essential, crucial insights and strategies for leaders to learn how to connect at deeper, more interpenetrating levels with those who follow their lead, and for the followers who take their lead. In fact, every leader needs those who can advance, refine, and execute their vision. The role that the followers play in any organization is tied to their participation at a level of advancement, refinement, and execution. As you read through these pages, you will discover the practical and strategic ways in which those who follow can make any organization achieve its intended greatness. I offer my highest accolades for Tracey's willingness to put these truths on the printed page. Whether you follow or whether you lead, this book will add significant value to your journey.

Mark J. Chironna, Ph.D.
The Master's Touch International Church
Mark Chironna Ministries
Orlando, Florida

Followership brings a much needed fresh perspective to leadership's clients—namely its followers! So much effort has been put into styles, methods, communicating, and even marketing the need of leadership, that seldom do we examine the actual leadership product. We ought to be producing good followers—who in turn become leaders who produce better followers. Tracey Armstrong, whom I consider both a mentor and one I mentor, has made the connection. Who's teaching us how to follow? What good is leadership training if those being trained haven't got a clue on how to follow? *Followership* is simply profound. Enjoy and explore the missing element no one is talking about, from someone who knows followership. Through my years of working with him and under him as a consultant to our organization, I know that his is the voice you must hear to connect the dots of leadership-followership.

Phil Munsey
Life Church
Irvine, California

TABLE of CONTENTS

Part Three: Lifestyle

Part Four: Follow the Leader

INTRODUCTION

The officer on whose arm the king was leaning said to the man of God, "Look, even if the Lord should open the floodgates of the heavens, could this happen?" "You will see it with your own eyes," answered Elisha, "but you will not eat any of it!" (2 Kings 7:2 NIV)

EVERY ORGANIZATION HAS THREE major needs in its chart: a driver, a developer, and a detailer. In the book *The E-Myth,* these three functions are the entrepreneur, the manager, and the technician.[1] The driver does exactly that: he or she drives the vision. The developer, who operates like a manager, develops and executes the vision. The detailer is the artist who produces the project. This is also seen in the Godhead. The Father says what He wants to happen, the Son administrates what the vision should look like, and the Holy Spirit manifests the vision. In order to be effective in ministry, business, sports, or family life, you must have these three in line and in unity. If you are what I call a *leader-servant,* someone who is called to execute the vision, you will fall into one of the above categories, and it is vitally important that you understand where you fit. The officer in Second Kings 7:2 was a developer. He should not have been trying to give directions in the meeting with Elijah; he should have allowed his leader to gain the full picture and saved his comments until the private counsel chambers. If he had not been so outspoken at the wrong time, he would have eaten with the rest of the city. A lot goes into being the man or woman upon whom the King leans.

Coach on the Floor

If you are the one that the leader leans on and counts on to get it done, then this book is for you! I learned these principles from the men and women I served, but they are not everyday lessons, nor are they taught openly. I learned some things from growing up with world-class athletes, from my previous religious experiences, from business, and from serving my mentors. I learned that there is an etiquette in being a follower or a leader-servant. A leader-servant is someone who leads with a servant attitude and serves with a leader's attitude. Our dilemma is that we have a lot of people who know how to lead and feel significant, yet we don't have a lot of people who know how to follow and feel significant. We teach people leadership before we teach them followership. I looked up the word *leadership* in the dictionary, and it is there, but the word *followership* is not. I realize that all of the great lessons of leadership I have gained came from direct experiences of following, not from a book on leadership. In order to be a great leader, you must first become a great follower. Michael Jordan was a leader on the basketball court, but he was great because of his followership.

When the Chicago Bulls basketball team regularly won championships, the coach, Phil Jackson, was asked, "What is the key? Michael Jordan, right?" "Yes, but not for the reason you may think," he replied. "Not for the scoring?" the reporter asked. "No," said Coach Jackson. "Not for playmaking?" "No." "It must be for his defense?" "No," Jackson responded to the reporter. "He was my coach on the floor. He executed my directions, the game plan, the way I wanted the team to play. He was the role model, the prototype player, and he ensured that the rest of the team modeled what I expected. He worked relentlessly to learn and elevate his play. He set an example for the team, being the last that left the floor in free throw practice and the first and last in and out of the weight room."[2]

Every leader needs a coach on the floor!

This book is about the servant's heart in an individual upon whom the king is able to lean. This is written for the person who believes in a leader and wants to walk alongside, assisting him or her in accomplishing the Father's business. It is also for those who have the heart of a Jonathan or Joseph, who feel called to being a second man or woman serving with all of their heart the lead man or woman. This is for the future leader who feels that nagging inner itch of greatness, and for the leader who needs help developing followers. My goal for writing this book is to help you keep from making the same mistakes I made and to give you the necessary balance between ministry and leadership. I have written it specifically for the person upon whom the king leans—to help you understand what your leader really needs from you and how to follow with a leadership focus.

No Reputation

Jesus did not come into the earth to be a leader. He constantly made it clear that He was here under the authority of His Father. Jesus came as a follower with a leadership perspective.

Jesus could have come in the same level as the Father, but He took a followership position with honor, to be an example of how we should live. Jesus was the ultimate leader-servant.

Let this mind be in you which was also in Christ Jesus, who, being in the form of God, did not consider it robbery to be equal with God, but made Himself of no reputation, taking the form of a bondservant, and coming in the likeness of men. And being found in appearance as a man, He humbled Himself and became obedient to the point of death, even the death of the cross. Therefore God also has highly exalted Him and given Him the name which is above every name (Philippians 2:5-9).

At first glance, leader-servants look like they are the leaders, yet they are the followers. They work hard at being so much like their leader that they take on the leadership characteristics of their leader. That is what Jesus did; He came in the form of man with the power and authority of God. Jesus humbled Himself and became obedient even to the point of death. The word *became* is very important to note. To *become* something takes much effort. Jesus put effort into becoming obedient, which means that He had a chance to not be obedient. The devil had a chance to be a leader-servant and decided that he would rather lead the whole thing than follow his Leader.

Choose to be of no reputation. Choose followership and let God raise you up. God exalts the humble and throws down the proud! (See First Peter 5:5-7.)

Endnotes

1. Michael E. Gerber, *The E-Myth: Why Most Businesses Don't Work and What to Do About It* (Pensacola, FL: Ballinger Pub. Co., 1985).

2. John C. Maxwell, *Winning With People: Discover the People Principles that Work for You Every Time* (Thomas Nelson, 2005).

PART 1

SPIRIT LED

CHAPTER ONE

EMBRACE THEIR SPIRITUAL AUTHORITY

MANY OF US ARE familiar with the story of the centurion who sought Jesus' help on behalf of his servant who lay sick. Jesus was impressed with the faith of the centurion; He knew that only a person with an understanding of submission and authority could have this kind of faith. We could examine this story from many angles regarding leadership. But let's take a moment to look at the story of the centurion from a follower's perspective:

> When Jesus had entered Capernaum, a centurion came to
> Him, asking for help. "Lord," he said, "my servant lies at
> home paralyzed and in terrible suffering." Jesus said to him,
> "I will go and heal him." The centurion replied, "Lord, I do
> not deserve to have you come under my roof. But just say the
> word, and my servant will be healed. For I myself am a man
> under authority, with soldiers under me. I tell this one, 'Go,'
> and he goes; and that one, 'Come,' and he comes. I say to my
> servant, 'Do this,' and he does it." When Jesus heard this, he
> was astonished and said to those following him, "I tell you

the truth, I have not found anyone in Israel with such great faith (Matthew 8:5-10 NIV).

What did you see? Did you see that the centurion was able to subject himself to Christ because he was someone who understood authority? I have seen good people lose miraculous moments and divine opportunities by not submitting to the authority at hand because of differences in personality, opinion, or tradition. The centurion could have used many excuses for why he would not submit to Jesus. He could have excused himself for reasons of race or culture, because he was a Roman soldier, or because their belief systems didn't match. If he had not been so desperate, he could have had this mind-set.

Fortunately, he truly loved and had genuine care for his servant, which drove him to lay down all fears and prejudice to see his servant set free. This leads me to the next follower that I want to focus on. What kind of servant was the man or woman at the centurion's home? I find it amazing that this leader was so desperate to see his servant helped that he was willing to break laws and cultural barriers. What kind of precious follower was he or she? The centurion couldn't see himself without this servant. The thought of loss gave him the determination to save his servant at the expense of his own reputation. This is a man who was accustomed to telling his servants to go and to come, do this or that, and they would accomplish it. This type of servant is indispensable. I have some people on my team who cause me to pray, "God send me 100 more of these." My wife and I would bend over backward for these servants. We are constantly looking for opportunities to bless, encourage, or promote them. There is a relationship between a leader and a follower in which the manner that the follower follows ministers immensely to the leader.

I wish that I could have seen the heart of service that the servant had that would cause the centurion to go out of his way to find help. I can only speculate on why this man went the extra mile for his servant. I can only lean on a few Scriptures that help me understand. First, we reap what we sow; possibly the centurion was only doing what he had been reaping. Whenever someone does something good for me, I always want to repay his or her kindness with an act of kindness. Possibly the centurion was reciprocating the many years of service he had previously received from his servant. Or possibly the leader was driven by brotherly love. The Scripture says there is one who sticks closer than a brother, and that one is someone who shows him or herself friendly (see Prov. 18:24).

I imagine that the servant found the perfect balance of respect for his authority, serving with confidence, loyalty, and love. The Bible tells us to let the greatest of all be the servant of all (see Matt. 23:11). Here we see the tables turned; the leader was served by someone great, which thus caused the leader to serve the greatest of all. Often following is seen as a place of weakness when in actuality it is the greatest place.

> *But Jesus called them to Himself and said, "You know that the rulers of the Gentiles lord it over them, and those who are great exercise authority over them. Yet it shall not be so among you; but whoever desires to become great among you, let him be your servant. And whoever desires to be first among you, let him be your slave—just as the Son of Man did not come to be served, but to serve, and to give His life a ransom for many"* (Matthew 20:25-28).

Serving Out of the Greatness Within

The gift of leading is found within serving. Serving must be done with the gift that is within. Every great person or leader has served, and it was the serving that released the gift of leading. There is greatness in each of us; the question is truly, "Are we willing to serve it out of us?" I understand more about what it is to lead from my days of serving. Still, to this day I find opportunities to serve. I serve my pastor, my mentors, my spiritual fathers, my congregation, my team, and especially my family. This enables me to recognize great future leaders through their current serving capacity. It also helps me stay fresh and free from being tainted by my place of authority. Never feel that a servant is weak. Again, Jesus says that serving is greatness. He never said that leading is greatness. I will take it even one step further by saying that we must serve our greatness: our God-given gifts and talents. We don't serve from a place of greatness; we give out the greatness that we have within us to others who can benefit from what we carry within. Serve your God with the greatness within, serve your lead person with the greatness within, serve your community with the greatness within, serve your church (which is God's answer to your city) with the greatness within, and serve your family with the greatness within.

Submitting to authority is a sign of greatness. In the past I've had to submit to leaders who I thought were wrong at the time. Often I wanted to leave them and go to some other place where I thought a leader would be better for my future or life. Yet each time God challenged me to stay, to serve, to be quiet, and learn. I have received incredible rewards for obeying that challenge. Actually, after finding myself in their shoes later, I discovered why they did what they did. I did the exact things that I earlier disagreed with, and it has saved my ministry and family life! Often as servants we think that we totally understand the big picture. In actuality, we cannot fully appreciate the current picture unless we add to our understanding our leader's position, pressure, responsibilities, and mission. Be a great person, serve the leader, and God will do great things for you and through you.

I want to encourage you with a few sure truths from the Book of Hebrews, which will transform your life. There are many truths found in the Word of God about submitting to authority, such as Romans 13:1-5. But I want to show you the benefits of submitting, obeying, and following. Let's look at Hebrews chapter 13:

Remember your leaders, who spoke the word of God to you. Consider the outcome of their way of life and imitate their faith (Hebrews 13:7 NIV).

Remember when you first saw... Remember when you first... Remember when you.... Every memory has a feeling connected to it. When the Bible asks us to remember, God is trying to trigger a certain feeling, which in turn will do one of two things.

In the case of remembering something favorable and positive, your positive feelings will create an emotional strength and confidence to proceed to the next instruction. In the case of remembering something that has injured you in the past, the feeling of conviction or correction will trigger a warning and hopefully prevent you from making the same mistake again. When God asks us to remember, He wants us to see, feel, and do something based upon the experience we are recalling. In this verse, we are challenged to remember our leaders: remember how they changed your life, remember how it felt to have someone speak into your life, remember how the Word of God transformed your thinking and changed your life choices and direction.

Sometimes you have to remember what someone has done for you in the past in order to keep serving them in the future. I have had people say as they have left serving me, "You have changed my life," or "I will never be the same." They thought that the life-changing experience that I was instrumental in was finished, but they left prematurely, only to cycle through life over and over again without progress. Several times I have done the same thing. I misunderstood the situation and left my place of serving, only to return later in humility and repentance to learn more from that same leader. I have realized that if someone has taught me something once, they are positioned to teach me something again, as long as they don't stop learning themselves. I did not always agree with everything that the leadership did, and I probably wouldn't even to this day agree completely with all of their philosophies, but that doesn't stop me from serving with them or serving them. It will never stop me from learning from them.

I have found that leaders are making constant changes personally, culturally, emotionally, and organizationally. This often leaves them without the proper balance or even without the words to describe how they feel or what they are going through. No one goes through more changes than a leader, because leadership is all about results, which demands constant change in every way in character, passion, and knowledge. If you as a servant are not careful, you could have a hard time adjusting and flexing with your leader's growth pattern and season of transition. During a season when you suspect that your leader is growing and transitioning, beware of judgments and unrealistic expectations. The best thing is to be watchful and prayerful; otherwise, you could be tempted to lose confidence in your leader. This is a grave mistake on the part of any servant. The leader will soon find his balance again, and the one who taught you and changed your life in the past will regain his confidence and yours as he feels your support and prayers. Transitioning from a lesser capacity to a greater capacity is a huge leadership shift for any pastor or businessperson.

You can actually help your leaders through this season by encouraging them with your testimony again. Remind them how they have changed your life. This is a major part of being a servant worthy to lean on in times and seasons of transition. All leaders need dynamic servants during these critical times of change that are so necessary if they are going to reach their full potential.

I realized that I needed my leaders again for the same life-changing words from God that had so impacted my life earlier. I try to keep these relationships nurtured because one word from the man or woman of God can transform my life again.

I need to consistently remind myself of how the leaders that God sent into my life lived and how they are growing into their next level. I don't want to be jealous or concerned that they are going to leave me behind, but I have made up my mind that wherever they go, I go, so that I can grow and reap the rewards of servanthood as Elisha did with Elijah. (See Second Kings 2:1-14.) When I have a struggle with them or their ideology, I remember how they have cared and the words that they have spoken over my life. I rehearse each spoken word in my mind and speak them out loud over my life. I remember these words whenever they are applicable to circumstances in my life or ministry. I remember the encouraging words and even the reprimands, which came only to make me a better person. I remember the preached words, which inspired me to live a godly and faith-filled life. Remember life lessons from your past, especially when your current situation is less than what you desire. This process will help you rekindle value into a relationship where value has been lost.

Considering Your Leader

The next thing that we see in Hebrews 13:7 is that we need to consider the lifestyle of our leaders. Take into account where your leader has been and where he or she is going. Is this where you desire to go? Is this how you desire to live? As a servant, it is your right to partake of the same favor and blessing experienced by the one you serve.

When things are going well, consider how thankful you are to be where you are, doing what you are doing, with your co-laborers. To "consider" involves having gratitude for the past, present, and future opportunities. Consideration is also what happens when you red dot your skills and talents as part of a team, building a great work and organization for God.

The writer of Hebrews instructs us to investigate our leadership relationship. This advice is good at any place of serving, in the enjoyable times and especially in the not-so-enjoyable times. Look again! Look again and again at their outcomes. Look not only at what they do that results in success, but also at their failures. These are equally valuable lessons to be learned. This doesn't mean to look at their failures with judgment in your heart; look at their shortcomings with grace and mercy as you seek to understand the pressures of leadership. Followers can make mistakes, and only a few will criticize them; yet, if a leader fails, almost all will criticize and mock. When you look again, look for the outcome of their character or the outcome of their joy, which is a fruit of the Spirit. Sometimes the outcome that we should look for is not a natural result but an emotional result or a confidence, a result from an increase in character. For example, a great leader and friend in my life is Pastor Phil Munsey. I have watched Phil for years lay down his life for the Gospel, sowing in one area and reaping in another. In his book *Legacy Now* he shares his inward battle of how it felt to be slowed down by the Sunday morning traffic of those who were headed to Saddleback Church, pastored by Rick Warren, a megachurch in the tens of thousands, while driving to his church of thousands. I have watched Phil maintain integrity and character while rejoicing with Rick as God blessed Saddleback. I have watched the way that Pastor Phil handled his personal struggles and how God has blessed him because he chose to rejoice instead of complain. God has blessed Pastor Phil with rich personal relationships with those who have, are, and will influence the world in a great way because of this same attitude that celebrates others' advancement and promotion. The favor that he lives under is a sign of success, which has no quantification. The honor that God has given Pastor Phil by allowing him to be an influence in the lives of great influencers is bestowed because he has developed an inward character that is both attractive and admirable.

Let's look at a different version of the same Scripture. The New King James Version reads as follows:

> *Remember those who rule over you, who have spoken the word of God to you, whose faith follow, considering the outcome of their conduct* (Hebrews 13:7).

This Scripture actually encourages us to follow their faith and consider their conduct. It doesn't give us the freedom of following only when we agree with their conduct, but we must follow their faith and consider the fruit of their behavior. Following is a decision of faith and not emotion. It is a decision to live in the will of God. If your leader is a spear thrower, don't throw spears back. Be led by the Spirit and directed by the words that you have heard. If your leader is a righteous man or woman, the Word of God commissions us to follow his or her faith, or confidence.

Let's go back to the previous version of Scripture that ends with the statement *"imitate their faith"* (NIV). A submitted person obeys what she knows is right by intentionally mimicking and imitating the faith of her leader. Imitate your leader's righteous behavior, imitate his controlled emotions, and imitate his achievements. This is a great insight. When I read this Scripture, it gave me confidence to believe that as my leaders go, so I go. My service will be rewarded. It is my right to excel as they are excelling. I have laid down my life and dreams in order to assist them in reaching their dreams and whatever God is calling them to achieve. I believe that I now can partake in their blessings and the fruit of their anointing.

When I went to Northern Ireland, I found myself pronouncing some of my words differently after a few days. Not on purpose but through association. When I returned to the United States, I found myself saying things that reminded me of being in Ireland. How much stronger would the accent increase if I did it intentionally! In the same manner you will have a certain level of success simply through associations, but how much more success would you experience through intentionally mimicking the anointing and faith of your leader? Those who have intentionally imitated my wife and I have grown and achieved beyond their peers in many ways. I believe that because I serve successful men and women of God I can operate in their anointing, as well as mine. That is one of the rewards of serving. We will look more closely at this concept in the last chapter.

Uncommon Submission

The only way to achieve true imitation is to live a life of obedience. Let's move further down the chapter to verse 17. When I first read this Scripture, it gripped me:

> *Obey those who rule over you, and be submissive, for they watch out for your souls, as those who must give account. Let them do so with joy and not with grief, for that would be unprofitable for you* (Hebrews 13:17).

As I read this verse, I was hit with the overwhelming responsibility to submit to my leader in an uncommon way. On the flip side, I was convicted to watch over the souls of those whom I lead in an uncommon way; one day I will have to answer for them, hopefully with joy in my heart and not pain. I knew that I must become both a better leader and a better follower. I surely didn't want those who would speak to the Lord on my behalf to have grief in their hearts as He asked them to tell Him about my obedience and submission. I want an awesome referral from my pastors as I enter into Heaven. I know that when I get to Heaven I will have to give God an account for the people who have moved from our ministry prior to their appointed time. God will ask me about their followership, and I will have to say I didn't know them because they wouldn't obey or submit to my authority. This will grieve God's heart as well as mine as I give my report card. Hebrews 13:17 clearly shows us this prospect: *"Obey those who rule over you, and be submissive, for they watch out for your souls, as those who must give account."*

Humanity has fought so hard for freedom and independence that it wants to do away with the words *obey* and *submit*. It seems that with every turn of the earth, independence becomes more and more like lawlessness or rebellion. I believe that this will be the dividing line between worldliness and Kingdom building. The Kingdom of God, like all civilizations, must be built upon some form of hierarchy. Lack of order breeds chaos. Without a chain of command, we would be living in the Wild West.

Everything that produces and grows must follow the laws of obedience and submission; churches, businesses, governments, schools, teams of any kind must have these two things. Even as I write these words *obedience* and *submission*, I feel that many will misunderstand my intentions. These words are not words of control but words of maturity, team spirit, and unity. For example, when I was young, I played on a peewee football team. One year the coach moved me from half back to wide receiver. I didn't mind the move, but I didn't take the change seriously, nor did I make the necessary changes in order to play the new position. Now the same plays meant something different to me in the receiver position. I knew what the halfback was going to do, but not the receiver. So when my leader needed me to be in the right place at the right time to throw the ball to me, I was not in position to receive the pass. Time after time this hindered the team from scoring because I was not positioned where the leader needed me to be. Had I studied and memorized the plays, it would have been an act of obedience for the team's sake, not just toward the leader. If I would have run the routes that the plays prescribed for me, I would have been submitting to the team and not only to the leader. Obedience and submission are big picture words for big picture thinkers!

When Hebrews 13:17 speaks of obedience and submission, it is actually encouraging us to become big picture thinkers and big team players. Much more rides on our victory than merely our egos or our feelings. You and I must learn the plays in the Kingdom playbook and run the patterns that have been strategically laid down for us to run. When we do, we will score a goal for the team, Team Kingdom of God.

It's All About Attitude

Does the Lord delight in burnt offerings and sacrifices as much as in obeying the voice of the Lord? To obey is better

than sacrifice, and to heed is better than the fat of rams
(1 Samuel 15:22 NIV).

Obedience is better than sacrifice—not because they are different
actions. They actually may be the same actions: Abraham was obedient
in offering his son Isaac as a sacrifice. Once he passed the test, God said,
"Now I know what is in your heart." Acts of obedience show what is in
your heart; it's a choice, it's an attitude, and it may even be voluntary. In the
Old Covenant, sacrifices were made out of necessity. Could it be that our
attitudes are more important to God than our actions? Yes, yes, yes! While
sacrificing, I could still have a bad attitude, and it may or may not affect
anything. Yet, if I have a bad attitude while trying to obey, it will pollute
my actions.

You may have heard it said, "Your attitude affects your altitude." I
believe I can safely say from this Scripture, "My attitude affects others'
altitude." "*Let* [your leaders rule over you]...*with joy and not with grief*"
(Heb. 13:17). Let them do so with joy, let them do so with *chara* (khar-
ah')—gladness, or calm delight.[1] I am encouraged when I talk to a person
who is happily married, and they are describing their relationship. Most
often tears and huge grins accompany their loving and adoring words. As I
see their joy, I say to myself, "They are really in love."

If God were to ask King David about the servanthood of Jonathan,
how would David answer God? How would Paul report to God regarding
Timothy? Would he answer with joy? Or would he be forced to answer
with grief in his heart? How would Paul answer to the Lord for John Mark?
We know that at one time, Paul refused to bring John Mark on a mission
trip because he left them at a crucial time on a previous trip. Fortunately
for John Mark, Paul gave him another chance to show himself approved
and a workman for the Kingdom of God (see 2 Tim. 2:15).

Showing Yourself Approved

I have had to make the return home to leaders I left prematurely. I had to go back and make it right until they were willing to send me and not just release me or tolerate my leaving. I humbled myself even when I thought that I was right in leaving, and God has been rewarding me ever since. Now I am confident that my leader will stand before God and will give a strong account on my behalf. When I was finally released from these ministries, these ministries also sent me. My wife and I have decided that if our mentors, pastor, or church won't send us, then we can't go. Submission is a jurisdiction and authority issue, not a feeling or agreeing issue. I have had people submit to me one week and tell me the following week that God told them to leave, while asking for our release and sending. I will not be able to give them a recommendation from my heart with joy because their decision to leave was not a decision of authority and submission. Jesus must give an account of Judas as the son of perdition.

> *While I was with them in the world, I kept them in Your name. Those whom You gave Me I have kept; and none of them is lost except the son of perdition, that the Scripture might be fulfilled* (John 17:12).

This was the accounting of Jesus to the Father of those whom He lost and those whom He kept. Jesus said the only one that He lost was the son of ruin or loss. No leader wants to say to God, I have lost the son of corruption. So often followers who start off right will end wrong because they become corrupted somewhere along the way. It may start off as a small disagreement with the vision, gossip, offense, or an unintentional embarrassment that sends the follower spinning into an uncontrolled frustration and dissatisfaction. The enemy is subtle in bringing his division. Don't allow any thoughts or feelings to go unresolved, for it will fester into corruption every time!

Your goal as a follower who desires to minister to your leader must be to give her joy in serving you as you serve her. If you create immediate joy in your leader's heart and mind, she will be excited about giving an account of your unselfish service in helping her reach Kingdom goals. Every leader will have to give an account of those who serve. What they will say in that account is up to you. Your leader's account of your submission will directly affect your future. The end of Hebrews 13:17 reads, *"for that would be unprofitable for you."* The Kingdom of God has a very strong reward system; for good work a laborer is rewarded greatly. There is also a reward system for the lack of work and bad work. This Scripture admonishes us to beware of the way we obey and submit to our leaders; it encourages us to obey and submit in such a way that they will give a good report to God on the day of judgment for us, because they watch over our souls. We will be rewarded by this report. The question is whether our reward is one of gain. In the last part of this book, we will talk about the gainful reward now and in eternity for a laborer who lives obediently, submitted to spiritual authority.

The Cost of Disobedience

Let's look at the destructive nature of disobedient and insubordinate attitudes. A verse in Samuel compares these mind-sets to the works of heathens:

> *For rebellion is as the sin of witchcraft, And stubbornness is as iniquity and idolatry. Because you have rejected the word of the Lord, He also has rejected you from being king* (1 Samuel 15:23).

The power of disobedience is so potent that it corrupted everything on earth at the fall of mankind. Adam and Eve were not the only ones who suffered from the fall. But every kingdom that is upon the earth has been affected and must be saved. The Bible says that all creation was subject to corruption because of the fall of man (see Rom. 8:20).

I appreciate the way the Message Bible presents 1 Samuel 15:23:

> *Not doing what God tells you is far worse than fooling around in the occult. Getting self-important around God is far worse than making deals with your dead ancestors. Because you said No to God's command, he says No to your kingship.*

Just think about this scripture for a moment… It would be better for a person to mess around with witchcraft than they should ever live in disobedience. Many people excuse their disobedience as a mere mistake and at the same time have a self-righteous attitude toward witches and warlocks. We must be careful to have a true evaluation of ourselves. The comparisons didn't stop at witchcraft. The Message Bible compares self-importance or stubbornness to worshiping the dead. Most people would never think of worshiping the dead. Yet we often justify many different levels of stubbornness with statements like, "I will do it, but I will do it my way or in my time."

An act of rebellion would be not doing what is asked by authority or ignoring what was asked and pretending that you didn't hear what was asked.

2 Corinthians 10:6 says that we will be ready to punish disobedience once we have fulfilled our obedience. The word *obedience* used in that passage means attentive hearing. So we must be willing to punish all inattentive hearing once we have fully accomplished what we hear and know.

In the Kingdom of God, authority is vitally important. Jurisdiction and reward for right and wrong deeds are vitally important for keeping order and peace. Obedience and submission are crucial to the growth of the Kingdom of Heaven.

Therefore submit yourselves to every ordinance of man for the Lord's sake, whether to the king as supreme, or to governors, as to those who are sent by Him for the punishment of evildoers and for the praise of those who do good. For this is the will of God, that by doing good you may put to silence the ignorance of foolish men — as free, yet not using liberty as a cloak for vice, but as bondservants of God. Honor all people. Love the brotherhood. Fear God. Honor the king (1 Peter 2:13-17).

This makes it very clear that we obey and submit to every kind of authority for the Lord's sake. We will open ourselves to the sin of lucifer if we forget why we choose to obey. We shouldn't simply submit because we want to or because we agree with the situation, but we must submit because the Lord wants us to. We must avoid justifying a lack of submission or obedience because we have a different opinion than the ordinance of man as the Bible calls it; we must submit to the ordinance of man because it's for the Lord's benefit. We often want to benefit God by doing something significant or mighty, when He may get just as much or more glory from how we submit to the authority and ordinance of man which He put in place.

Let every soul be subject to the governing authorities. For there is no authority except from God, and the authorities that exist are appointed by God. Therefore whoever resists the authority resists the ordinance of God, and those who resist will bring judgment on themselves. For rulers are not a terror to good works, but to evil. Do you want to be unafraid of the authority? Do what is good, and you will have praise from the same. For he is God's minister to you for good. But if you do evil, be afraid; for he does not bear the sword in vain; for he is God's minister, an avenger to execute wrath on him who practices evil. Therefore you must be subject, not only because of wrath but also for conscience' sake. For because of this you also pay taxes, for they are God's ministers attending continually to this very thing. Render therefore to all their due: taxes to whom taxes are due, customs to whom customs, fear to whom fear, honor to whom honor (Romans 13:1-7).

WOW! Believers all around the world are in danger of bringing judgment upon themselves by resisting the ordinance of God. Isn't it interesting that in this scripture the ordinance of man is now referred to as the ordinance of God? Becoming familiar with authority is very dangerous. In the same manner being afraid of authority is dangerous. You may ask, "Why?" Because authority is in place to protect the just from the unjust, if you are just, you will be at peace with the ordinance of God. If you are unjust, then you should be afraid. God gives us authorities in our lives to minister as avengers against all who practice unrighteousness.

The way you and I submit actually reveals our conscience. Our submission not only benefits the Lord but it also benefits our conscience. And let me tell you, there is no better living than living with a clear conscience.

In a society where ministers are trying to be relevant, parents are trying to befriend their kids, and officials are getting very little respect, the word *honor* is getting very little time on our lips. We must bring honor back to our homes. If we don't honor earthly authority such as parents, ministers, or officials, how could we really honor God? I believe that if Adam and Eve had shown greater honor for God, they would have heeded His words and would have placed so much importance on what He said that no one would have been able to mislead them. I believe that we must honor God by submitting to the ordinance of man for the Lord's sake and the benefit of our conscience.

True Authority

A righteous person understands that God has placed all leaders or authorities in the position that they hold for reasons that only He understands. The key for us is to honor God by honoring His ministers to whom He has given jurisdiction. When God speaks, He deals in the realm of jurisdictional authority. When God speaks to a family, God wants to speak to the head of the house. In cases such as a single mother or father, God speaks to the head *in* the house. God desires to speak to the man of the house, but He desires to speak to the rest of the household as well. God speaks to my wife as much or sometimes even more than He does to me. Yet God doesn't bypass my authority in the house to speak to my wife without letting me know the direction that He is setting. God speaks to me as the head of the house, and at the same time speaks to my wife as the heart of the family. The head cannot make good decisions without including the heart. When the head of the house and the heart of the house come together to hear God's direction, it is a powerful thing to see true authority take its place and rule the family together. Ultimately, as the man of the house, I am accountable for the decision that we make as a team.

True authority never wants to control or manipulate. True authority desires to partner and team up with others in order to maximize and multiply their strengths for a better result.

When God speaks to the local church, He wants to speak to the head of that local church and the team He has gathered to lead. God doesn't speak directionally to anyone and everyone in the church regarding the direction of the organization. If He does share something with the rest of the congregation, it is for the sake of prayer, fasting, and following. The purpose is not for splitting, separating, or leading sheep away. Things go desperately wrong when the line of authority gets blurred. You may have a sense of the direction as a follower, but God will still demand obedience, honor, and submission from you until you are asked to take the lead by the leader on the job.

A Joyful Relationship

I like the way Hebrews chapter 13 ends: *"Greet all those who rule over you, and all the saints"* (Heb. 13:24). After all of the communication on how to relate to authority as an obedient and submissive worker in the Kingdom, this chapter finishes with a clear picture that obedience and submission should not destroy the approachability and accessibility of the leader. This shows that a leader-follower relationship should be a relationship of joy and enthusiasm, not a relationship of intimidation or control. I take pleasure in the greeting of co-laborers who enjoy serving with us in ministry. Their eyes brighten up and smiles come upon their faces when they see my wife and me. In return, Nathalie and I enjoy seeing them; their greetings change our countenance. The Bible says it this way:

> *A merry heart makes a cheerful countenance, but by sorrow of the heart the spirit is broken* (Proverbs 15:13).
>
> *As iron sharpens iron, so a man sharpens the countenance of his friend* (Proverbs 27:17).

With this in mind, be aware of how you greet your leader. Your greeting can encourage them or discourage them. If you truly desire to minister to your leader, consider how you would want to feel if someone that you were leading greeted you. To minister to them is to serve them. Serve them with your intentional joy, your overcoming confidence, the surety of loyalty, your "whatever-it-takes-faith," and a "go-the-extra-mile-attitude."

Endnote

1. "Chara"; http://www.studylight.org/lex/grk/view.cgi?number=5479.

CHAPTER TWO

BE SPIRITUALLY HUNGRY

Meanwhile, the disciples were urging Jesus to eat. "No," he said, "I have some food you don't know about." "Who brought it to him?" the disciples asked each other. Then Jesus explained: "My nourishment comes from doing the will of God who sent me, and from finishing his work"
(John 4:31-34 TLB).

HUNGER CREATES A VACUUM that demands to be filled. If you don't eat, you will crave food, and that craving will cause you to look for something that will satisfy. If the cravings are not satisfied, they will only increase, until eventually you will eat whatever you can find. Hunger is a sign that the body is in need of nourishment. These disciples were doing the right thing for their leader; they wanted to make sure that He was nourished physically.

Jesus said, *"I have some food you don't know about."* Of course Jesus was talking about the will of God for His life. There was something on the heart of this leader that His disciples just couldn't understand, live in, or receive. Jesus referred to the will of God for His life as *food*. There was a craving in His life to do something that others didn't know about. As disciples of a leader, you too must have a burden to carry that which others will not understand.

Peter had a different hunger than John. John 21:20-23 reads:

> *Then Peter, turning around, saw the disciple whom Jesus loved following, who also had leaned on His breast at the supper, and said, "Lord, who is the one who betrays You?" Peter, seeing him, said to Jesus, "But Lord, what about this man?" Jesus said to him, "If I will that he remain till I come, what is that to you? You follow Me." Then this saying went out among the brethren that this disciple would not die. Yet Jesus did not say to him that he would not die, but, "If I will that he remain till I come, what is that to you?"*

The hunger of the Lord is personal, because hunger for the things of God is the reason some people run a little harder and more passionately than other believers. The way we pursue the Lord may be different from others, but one can never pursue devoid of passion. We see in the passage above two individuals who had incredible passions for their leader, yet they displayed them differently. There is no question whether both Peter and John loved Jesus. But John, the one who was called *beloved,* had a different pursuit. His pursuit found him intimately interacting with the Lord. As the scripture says, he *"leaned on His breast at the supper."* To lean on the chest of someone is very personal, close, and intimate. John's pursuit was to be close to his leader. Peter's pursuit was to perform for the leader.

Peter's performance-driven pursuit lacked intimacy and love. We see that from when Peter wanted to walk on the water, and when he chopped off a soldier's ear. Peter was a fighter and John was a lover. In the end, Jesus challenged Peter to love, which is what he needed to learn if he was going to be the rock of the Church. However, no leader needs just lovers around them. Lovers with no fight are no good to the cause, yet doers without love and intimacy are hard and destructive. Followership demands the beautiful balance of intimacy and doing. Growing in new areas is not easy, but the truth of the matter is that every one of us must pick up our cross and follow Christ.

The drive to do the will of God and finish it must come from a heart that knows the perfect will of God for our lives. A lack of passion and luster comes from not knowing the personal and perfect will of God.

The lack of knowledge brings destruction, according to Hosea 4:6:

> *My people are destroyed for lack of knowledge: because thou*
> *hast rejected knowledge, I will also reject thee...* (KJV).

If the lack of knowledge is the cause of destruction, then the possession of knowledge is the power of construction.

> *Then said Jesus to those Jews which believed on Him, "If*
> *ye continue in My word, then are ye My disciples indeed"*
> (John 8:31 KJV).

Knowing the will of God empowers us to do what we are destined to do and finish. The will of God is finding, doing, and finishing what God has determined from the beginning of time for your life. Knowing the will of God gives you the freedom, energy, and faith to walk out the will of God. The more a person knows of what he is destined to do, the more desire and energy he will have to work and to achieve whatever is desired. Whatever consumes your attention drives your passion.

Spiritual hunger will never be satisfied until the will of God is finished. One of the most important things to a leader is that they have people around them with spiritual hunger. Spiritual hunger will cause a worker to find new ways to do the will of God. Spiritual hunger will cause a servant to answer questions before the leader has the need or chance to ask. Spiritual hunger causes you to rise to the level that God demands from you.

So how do you generate spiritual hunger? First, there must be dissatisfaction with what you already know. There must be a craving for a greater knowledge of the will of God for your life. True heartfelt dissatisfaction will create such a void that it will cause you to seek the Lord on how to satisfy the emptiness.

Jesus was nourished from doing the will of God: *"My nourishment comes from doing the will of God who sent Me"* (John 4:34 NLT). How do you find the will of God? You find the will of God by having a *P.R.O.* life. *P* for prayer, *R* for reading the Word daily, and *O* for obeying God at all times.

Nourishing A Strong Prayer Life

Without a daily prayer life you will never have the sensitivity to the Lord to obey His leading and to follow the leader that He has sent into your life. Prayer keeps us humble and fresh as we seek to do the will of God.

There are two forms of prayer that your leader will benefit from as you incorporate them into your daily life. The first is devotional prayer. Devotional prayer should be exercised every day. An easy pattern for your devotional prayer time is to pray the Lord's Prayer. By praying each stage of the Lord's Prayer, you will pray through every category of life. Another pattern of prayer is found in Philippians 4:6:

> *Be anxious for nothing, but in everything by prayer and supplication, with thanksgiving, let your requests be made known to God.*

Frustration or anxiety calls for a need to seek God for answers. We are encouraged to be anxious for nothing. Don't allow any circumstances to drive you into a state of fear. Keep an atmosphere of faith in your personal life, in your work life, in your ministry life, in your business, conversation, and ministry. Keep the faith no matter how the circumstances may appear. Your leader needs you to live by faith and not by sight. There are times when you will need ministry from your leader, and most leaders who are led by God will look forward to the opportunity to minister to you when the need arises.

Gain confidence by overcoming anxiety through prayer, supplication, and with thanksgiving. I find that when I am pressing through to the next level, sometimes anxiety and fear try to take over my thought life. The way I overcome is by going to God, all the while knowing that He wants me to make my prayers and requests known to him. Anxiety will always be removed when seeking God.

As a leader, I appreciate those on my team whom I can count on being confident through the storm. There have been many times that as I was challenged by budget concerns or building projects or weak areas in the organization or the team, I found myself looking for eye contact from those at my table who had confidence on which I could feed. Let your leader feed on your confidence during times of challenge. Sometimes your confidence will be enough for them to press on to the next level and get a creative thought that will bring the organization higher. You will minister to your leader through your walk of confidence.

Posture yourself in prayer through praise and declaration that God is able. Start your prayer with the fact that *God can* do all things. Pray earnestly that God is the Author and Finisher of your faith. Then continue your prayer time with supplication; this is petitioning God for any request that will satisfy whatever causes anxiety. During this time of prayer, you will appeal to the mercy of God by involving Him in your life and needs. Supplicate with the mind-set that *God will* do all things according to His will. Finally, close this time of prayer with thanksgiving. Never walk away from the presence of God without thanking Him. You opened with prayer, you supplicated with confidence, and you'll finish with thankful worship. This part of the prayer time is to declare that *God has* done all that you have asked and you are thankful for it.

Praying in this way allows you to stay free of fear each and every day. You can go through the different categories of your life keeping the rhythms of *God can, God will,* and *God has.* Your devotional categories should include prayers dealing with your relationship with God, and with family, recreation, health, finances, business, and ministry. Also add a time of intercession to your daily devotions. Intercession is to pray on behalf of someone else. During intercession include prayers for those who rule over you.

All leaders need the prayers of those whom they govern; this includes both the saved and secular. You can also ask the Holy Spirit to help you in prayer for your leaders, and He will work with you in praying the will of God. We see this in Romans 8:26-27:

> *Likewise the Spirit also helps in our weaknesses. For we do not what we should pray for as we ought, but the Spirit Himself makes intercession for us with groanings which cannot be uttered. Now He who searches the hearts knows what the mind of the Spirit is, because He makes intercession for the saints according to the will of God.*

Lean on the Holy Spirit to help you pray effective prayers. Your intercession for your leader will help them to do and complete the will of God. As helpers, we should never complain about our leaders or what we think they are doing wrong, because God has given us the power to pray and bring about change. Of course, these prayers will only be effective when founded in love and a desire for nothing but the will of God.

Epaphras, who is one of you, a bondservant of Christ, greets you, always laboring fervently for you in prayers, that you may stand perfect and complete in all the will of God (Colossians 4:12).

Your leader can only stand perfect and complete in the will of God with your support. Stay supportive always, and you will be rewarded in this world and in the world to come. Also look at First Thessalonians 5:16-18, which reads:

Rejoice always, pray without ceasing, in everything give thanks; for this is the will of God in Christ Jesus for you.

Again, we see prayer as a part of the will of God. If you desire the will of God: pray, pray, pray!

Meditation as Prayer

Another form of prayer is meditation. I cannot stress this strongly enough; find time daily for the lost prayer form of meditation. Meditate as Philippians 4:8-9 teaches:

Finally, brethren, whatever things are true, whatever things are noble, whatever things are just, whatever things are pure, whatever things are lovely, whatever things are of good report, if there is any virtue and if there is anything praiseworthy—meditate on these things. The things which you learned and received and heard and saw in me, these do, and the God of peace will be with you.

Meditation has two meanings in the New Testament. One means to take inventory (see Phil. 4:8). Take inventory and think deeply about whatever things are true in your life, whatever things are noble, whatever things are just, whatever things are pure, whatever things are lovely, whatever things are of good report, if there is any virtue and if there is anything praiseworthy in your life. The second form of meditation is to take an image, either God inspired or inspired by the written word, and revolve it in your mind, imagining that you are living and becoming what you see (see 1 Tim. 4:15). You can find more information on meditation in my book, *Becoming a Pioneer of Success* published by Destiny Image. Meditation is a vital part of progressive Christian living.

Hunger for the Word

Along with prayer, you must have a life in the Word. Become a reader of the Word of God and other books that will help you develop. As you read the Word of God, make sure that you ask the Holy Spirit to teach you about what you are reading. The more you discover in the Word of God, the more excited you will get about reading the Word. Also remember that the more questions you ask as you read the Word, the more answers you will receive! The Word of God is living and practical; there will always be wisdom and insight for everyday life.

Word studies and specific topic searches will generate strength. I have done studies on healing, on leadership, on family, on child rearing, etc. There is truly no limit to what you will learn if you get hungry for the Word of God. At one stage in my study of the Word, it helped me to take a red highlighter and underline all the Scriptures that were promises for life. I called them power Scriptures. Jump into the Word with hunger, excitement, and expectation; you will be happy with the results. The Word of God helps us understand God and His ways. We will never know God's personality without finding out how He thinks. A healthy prayer life and Word life will help you discover how God thinks and what He desires.

Proving the Will of God

The last part of *P.R.O.* is doing the will of God. It is not an emotional thing; what you and I want comes secondary to what God desires. So we must change our way of thinking to match God's way. If we desire to know God's thoughts, we must be willing to seek His thoughts. At the same time we must be prepared to abandon any thoughts and beliefs that would contradict His thoughts and plans. In order to walk in God's ways, we need to conform to His ways.

> *And do not be conformed to this world, but be transformed by the renewing of your mind, that you may prove what is that good and acceptable and perfect will of God* (Romans 12:2).

The only way to prove the will of God is to immediately stop any actions which conform to the ways of the world and contradict the purposes of God. We also must change the way that we think in order to confirm the good, acceptable, and perfect determination of God. The perfect will of God is for us to live a life of abundance.

Years ago my wife went to get her blood work done. The nutritionist who did the blood work looked at it and embraced my wife in her arms to comfort her. My wife's blood work showed how physically fatigued she was. The blood spoke very loud to the doctor, who could tell that we lived in a highly polluted area—at that time we lived in Southern California. It showed deformed blood cells which had been damaged by fast food and by foods that had been cooked by microwaves. At the time, we traveled three weeks out of the month, which we thought forced us to eat fast food. The blood work also showed a high amount of cancer cells, which the doctor informed us that everybody has, but not so many that couldn't be defeated by healthy white blood cells. She knew our whole lifestyle by looking under a microscope at my wife's blood. She suggested that we change our diet immediately in order to save my wife's life, in actuality, both of our lives.

So we started to declare that God wanted us to eat for life and not just for taste. Whenever we would see a commercial that showed our favorite food, we would say, "How gross, look at that cancer on a bun!" Our taste buds were saying something totally different, but we forced a change in our actions by changing the way we saw the food. It was no longer "yummy," but it had to become "gross" and destructive in order for us to overcome the desire to eat it.

We will only overcome what we hate. In order to live a life full of abundance we must live a life that loves God's will and hates anything that keeps us from the perfect will of God. I have used this tool many times to overcome many things. The word *will* in its original context is a Greek-based word meaning "a desire, choice, or inclination"; this means that God has already made up His mind about you and for you.[1] We must do everything within our power to carry out what God has determined, chosen, or decided in His heart. Whatever God has determined will be done; it is up to us to choose whether or not we want to be a willing part of His plan.

If you are to choose the will of God, you first need to choose to know it. This hunger to know the will of God creates a desire for certainty, which results in the powerful motivations of frustration and dissatisfaction. These come when you don't have certainty of what the will of God is for your life. Highly motivated, you will then do anything to discover the perfect will of God for your life.

The will of God is totally purpose driven; it takes true energy and effort to find, do, and finish your purpose. For example, if I am craving savory food and I eat sweets, the craving for savory foods will still remain, even though I have filled my stomach with sweets. My craving for the savory will only be satisfied with savory. The search for the will of God is really the search for purpose. The kind of hunger that possesses you is a clue to the purposes of God that will nourish your life. As you hunger to live purposefully, you will find what God has said about you when He created all things. God spoke purpose, and the purpose that He spoke came into existence and took on whatever form necessary to achieve what God said. So hungering to know your purpose, together with seeking God to know His perfect determination for your life, will result in doing and finishing the will of God. You must be intellectually curious about what you are to become. Intellectual curiosity comes from passions that cause you to think deeply about who you are, who you serve, and how to do what you do better. You must also think deeply about who you associate with and why you endure any pain connected with your destiny. So often we talk about the emotions and feelings of passion, but there are some very real things happening in your thoughts as you live zealously. Passion will cause you to ask probing questions; these questions will cause you to seek out answers, and in turn you will find the determination of God.

The internal questions that we ask make a huge difference in the action that we take. For example, there is a difference between "Why did this happen to me?" and "What can I learn from this situation?" or "I don't like this situation! What will happen if I don't do anything about this situation?" The answer to that question will force you to look for a solution. We must avoid questions that form excuses; we must form questions in our mind that force change and action. One day I was asking a question in prayer, and for many, many days I felt as if I didn't get any clarity. Finally, I sensed the Holy Spirit saying, "You are asking the wrong question, so you won't get the right answer." So I changed my question from a "When will this happen?" to a "How can I make this happen?" and the answer came quickly. It's a concept similar to the difference between giving someone a fish or teaching him to fish. One way keeps a person wondering for more answers, and the other allows a person to take charge of his destiny.

Executing the Will of God

Simply knowing the will of God did not nourish Jesus; He was nourished from doing and finishing the will of God. The more He did, the more His curiosity was fulfilled. We must choose to get excited about executing the will of God. The will of God must be done, not simply seen or heard or known or felt or hoped for or sought after. In order to finish something, we must have constant action and energy toward it. Jesus made this clear to us in Mark 3:33-35 when He asked,

> *"Who is My mother, or My brothers?" And He looked around in a circle at those who sat about Him, and said, "Here are My mother and My brothers! For whoever does the will of God is My brother and My sister and mother."*

So many disciples get frustrated when their leaders desire for them to work hard for the Kingdom, do more for the Kingdom, and achieve more for the Kingdom. This frustration is only because they hunger for things other than the purposes of God and His Kingdom. Here, Jesus actually redefines His relationships and *only* includes those who do the will of God. Jesus only desired to associate with those who were purpose driven and had an orientation toward the will of God. The only exception was when Jesus was found associating with unsaved people; He fraternized with the lost in order to give them the opportunity to be converted and submitted to His leadership. But the standard was different for those who called Him Lord; He had very specific demands for them as followers. The key to being a follower of Christ is that you must be willing to do the will of God.

Not only should we do the will of God, but we should also finish it.

> *And whoever does not bear his cross and come after Me cannot be My disciple. For which of you, intending to build a tower, does not sit down first and count the cost, whether*

he has enough to finish it — lest, after he has laid the foundation, and is not able to finish, all who see it begin to mock him, saying, "This man began to build and was not able to finish" (Luke 14:27-30).

This Scripture encourages us to build with the cost figured in. When you make a commitment to serve someone or to take a position, count the cost before you make your final decision. Because once your choice is made, God will hold you responsible to finish it in order to be fit for the Kingdom of God.

> *No one, having put his hand to the plow, and looking back, is fit for the kingdom of God* (Luke 9:62).

According to Proverbs, slothfulness is akin to destruction (see Prov. 18:9). Slothful people don't plan, strategize, count the cost, or finish. Finishing is more than a decision to do it; it is a determination to complete the work! In order to finish, you must match your resolve to finish with God's strength of character. God's strength and character is dominant. When His garden project experienced a bump in the road, He executed the plan that would dominate and push through the bump. God's resolve is that there is always a way to make it work, no matter what obstacles present themselves. The word *quit* is not in the vocabulary of God. Without the perseverance to finish, quitting comes so easily. Could you imagine what would have happened if Christ had stopped during times of persecution and temptation, or in the Garden of Gethsemane? What if He had stated, "This is just too hard," and asked to get off the cross?

When you feel like giving up, follow the advice in Hebrews 12:3-4: *"For consider Him who endured such hostility from sinners against Himself, lest you become weary and discouraged in your souls. You have not yet resisted to bloodshed, striving against sin."* The next time you consider quitting before you have finished, think on the price that was paid for your freedom. Let the Author and Finisher of your faith give you the confidence to finish.

Build with an eternal perspective; anything less is a mockery to the Kingdom of God. Acts 13:36 says, *"For David, after he had served his own generation by the will of God, fell asleep."* Build with a heart for your generation. Find your place in serving your leader and your generation; this is the will of God. There is something inside of you that your generation needs; find it, actively do it, and finish it; this is the determination of God. When you reach the point where your dream is bigger than yourself, serving your generation and the one to come, you will live in an unquenchable fervor, an unstoppable drive, and an all-consuming hunger for the will of God for others. This kind of spiritual hunger will encourage the leader in you to serve, dream big, and think big as you count the cost of the will of God for your life.

Endnote

1. "Thelema"; http://www.studylight.org/lex/grk/view.cgi?number=2307.

CHAPTER THREE

SPIRITUAL ENTHUSIASM

For He put on righteousness as a breastplate, and a helmet of salvation on His head; He put on the garments of vengeance for clothing, and was clad with zeal as a cloak (Isaiah 59:17).

BEING AN ENTHUSIASTIC PERSON has nothing to do with personality. Enthusiasm is something that we all must put on. We must put on the zeal of the Lord, and we must put on enthusiasm as a cloak. When a warrior goes to war, he has to put on enthusiasm. He has to get pumped, no matter what his personality is like. The shy and introverted must still put on zest and excitement for the cause. Stirring up enthusiasm is a choice. Let zeal cover everything that you do. When you put it in your mind to serve, you must also put in your mind that there is no serving without enthusiasm.

Allow God to possess you as you set out to achieve your dreams. Don't believe the lie that your personality won't allow you to be enthusiastic. *Enthusiasm* means "belief in special revelations of the Holy Spirit; religious fanaticism; strong excitement of feeling; something inspiring zeal or ferver."[1] Here's a more detailed word history of *enthusiasm*:

"Nothing great was ever achieved without enthusiasm," said the very quotable Ralph Waldo Emerson, who also said, "Everywhere the history of religion betrays a tendency to enthusiasm." These two uses of the word *enthusiasm*—one positive and one negative—both derive from its source in Greek. *Enthusiasm* first appeared in English in 1603 with the meaning "possession by a god." The source of the word is the Greek *enthousiasmos*, which ultimately comes from the adjective *entheos*, "having the god within," formed from *en*, "in, within," and *theos*, "god." Over time the meaning of *enthusiasm* became extended to "rapturous inspiration like that caused by a god" to "an overly confident or delusory belief that one is inspired by God," to "ill-regulated religious fervor, religious extremism," and eventually to the familiar sense "craze, excitement, strong liking for something." Now one can have an enthusiasm for almost anything, from water skiing to fast food, without religion entering into it at all.[2]

Even though the word *enthusiasm* is used for doing anything that a person gets excited about or enjoys doing, its origin is found in serving God. The thing that we should understand is that people can get enthusiastic about watching a football game, yet struggle with enthusiasm about serving the house of God, the Kingdom of God, or the man or woman of God. How can we get enthusiastic about going golfing or fishing and not get enthusiastic about praising God? David said in Psalm 69:9, *"Zeal for Your house has eaten me up."* Be more enthusiastic about your involvement in the work of the Kingdom than about anything else.

My enthusiasm for my wife and children causes me to want to spend all of the time that I can find with them. The zeal that I have for God, His house, and His Kingdom causes me to want to spend all of my energy on Him, doing His will. My two greatest enthusiasms in life are serving my God and serving my family. These two relationships consume the majority of my time. What I am saying is that whatever has your enthusiasm has your time and attention. You will make time and room for whatever you decide to be enthusiastic about.

Generating Enthusiasm

Enthusiasm is a mind-set of willingness; a choice that you make. You may have to see yourself differently in order to stir the passions of enthusiasm. Start seeing yourself as a person who is able to create an excitement around everything that you do. Imagine that you are standing before God and He is very pleased at what you are doing for Him. Think on things that will bring joy and generate enthusiasm. You will have to develop the willingness to do this when you don't have it. What you see is what you get. Imagine an exciting, inspiring scene—as you do so, your nervous system activates feelings of excitement and enthusiasm, resulting in a motivation to pursue that very picture by any means necessary. In the same manner, imagine an unpleasant scene—a picture that is disappointing or discouraging. Eventually your nervous system will create a negative feeling that will cause you to make a judgment call that leads you to find ways to avoid this unpleasant picture and the accompanying feelings.

Stacking

You may want to try what I call "stacking." Stacking is a way to create enthusiasm in boring or unpleasant areas of your life and be motivated all of the time. Stacking borrows the emotion from one thing that you like to do and uses it in another thing that you don't enjoy. For instance, I enjoy studying. I like to study the Word of God. I like to study church and organizational leadership. I like to study success and wealth-building principles. I get enthusiastic about these things; I get energized when I find time to read a new book or listen to a new teaching series.

What I find less enjoyable is physical exercise, although I know I need to do it. I often feel like I could be doing something else. To be completely honest, sometimes I just don't feel like going into the gym, changing my clothes, working out, showering, getting dressed, and then going on with my day, a two-and-half-hour process. I saw this as a price that wasn't worth the results until I started stacking the two things: studying—which I was enthusiastic about; and working out—which I knew was necessary. By taking a teaching tape or a book on the subjects that I enjoyed, I found myself getting excited and enthusiastic about working out. I didn't realize what I was doing until one day I got to the gym and forgot my study materials. I worked out that day, but I didn't enjoy it as I normally did. I began to ask questions, which led me to stacking. I only enjoyed working out because it was an extra time of studying that I could sneak in daily. Suddenly I was getting the results that I wanted physically, mentally, emotionally, and spiritually. Stacking, refocusing on the positive, and meditating objectively will help you develop a willing mind. A willing mind will cause you to live a zealous life that others will be attracted to and desire to emulate.

> *...for I know your willingness, about which I boast of you*
> *to the Macedonians, that Achaia was ready a year ago; and*
> *your zeal has stirred up the majority* (2 Corinthians 9:2).

Enthusiasm is contagious. Let your zeal stir up the whole organization. As a leader I like to have enthusiastic people around me. They help me create an environment of excitement. When I ask for questions in a staff or leadership meeting, the enthusiasm of these people will always create a question and a conversation that all can learn from.

Enthusiastic followers have a curiosity that every leader needs to have around. The disciples didn't leave their boats and families simply because it was the right thing to do. They left for two reasons: first of all, Isaiah 9:7 says that God will bring forth increase through *the zeal of the Lord:*

Of the increase of His government and peace there shall be no end, upon the throne of David, and upon His kingdom, to order it, and to establish it with judgment and with justice from henceforth even forever. The zeal of the Lord of hosts will perform this (KJV).

The zeal of Christ caused people at work to leave their nets and money-collecting in order to follow Him; that is the power of zeal! Yet, the zeal of a leader can only affect those who are curious. And that is the second reason the disciples were willing to leave all they possessed to follow Christ: they were *intrigued* by His enthusiasm. Stay curious, and you will maintain enthusiasm. Your enthusiasm will draw curious people to assist you in your work and to follow your leadership. It's your choice to be possessed with the things of God and your decision to live enthusiastically.

Endnotes

1. *Merriam-Webster's Collegiate Dictionary*, 11th ed., s.v., "Enthusiasm."

2. See http://dictionary.reference.com/browse/enthusiasm.

CHAPTER FOUR

HIGHER LIVING

And he must have a good reputation with those outside the church, so that
he will not fall into reproach and the snare of the devil
(1 Timothy 3:7 NASB).

A GOOD REPUTATION COMES from a desire to have a good name. When someone speaks your name, what is the reaction of those who hear it? Is there anyone in your organization who can validly speak negatively of your name? Is there any reproach that can fall on you? Protect your name by keeping a good reputation. Your leader needs you to be a representation of the organization you serve, the Kingdom you serve, and the God you serve.

It is more important for you and me to have a free and clear name than to have all of the fame or money in the world. A few years ago I went to purchase a car. After filling out the credit application, the salesman came back to me with a huge smile on his face. He enthusiastically said, "Mr. Armstrong, you have great credit!" I looked at him like, "Should I have anything *other* than great credit?" He saw the question on my face and replied, "We have ministers come in all the time with horrible credit." He had the impression that ministers don't pay their bills and therefore have horrible credit. As a young man, I was refused many things because I didn't have credit. One day I got a credit card and didn't pay it off; it affected my credit and put me in a worse state than having no credit at all. So, from that time I realized that my name could buy me more than what my money could. Keeping my name without reproach was more valuable than having silver or gold.

The Word of God says this in Proverbs 22:1: *"A good name is to be chosen rather than great riches, loving favor rather than silver and gold,"* and in Ecclesiastes 7:1, *"A good name is better than precious ointment."* Protect your name at all costs. It will be no good for you or the Kingdom of God for you to be known as a thief, liar, gossip, sexually impure person, or any other reproachable identity. It is not worth the destruction that will follow or the pain that it will cause to the Kingdom of God.

There are unsaved people who need to see your Christian lifestyle. The work of God already suffers attack by the kingdom of darkness; we don't need any more attacks based upon a bad reputation. The enemy will snare others through any reproachable behavior in our lives. Living above reproach keeps in mind the people who would be hurt by our disgrace. There are people whom God is sending to you to reach; they will be hindered from hearing the Gospel if your name is tainted.

> And he must have a good reputation with those outside the church, so that he will not fall into reproach and the snare of the devil (1 Timothy 3:7 NASB).

This means as a righteous man or woman every action and deed must be filtered through the thought of "What would my unsaved next-door neighbor think about this action?" or "Could my unsaved boss receive the Gospel from me if I do this?" Keep an eternal perspective. Think: "How will this action affect the eternity of those who will be a part of it, hear about it, or see it?"

Of Good Reputation

As a leader, I am looking to get involved with people who will not bring unnecessary reproach to the work, the Kingdom, God, my family, or my life. I believe that the early apostles had the same thing in mind when they set the standard for those who would rise from discipleship into the ranks of deacon.

> *Therefore, brethren, seek out from among you seven men of good reputation, full of the Holy Spirit and wisdom, whom we may appoint over this business…* (Acts 6:3).

The first decisive factor was a good reputation. All of these factors are important for a worker to possess: good reputation, fullness of the Holy Spirit, and wisdom. Often the Bible will list things according to their priority. If a person doesn't care about their reputation, then he or she will not be willing to yield to the instruction of the Holy Spirit and live by principles of wisdom. A person who is truly filled with the Holy Spirit and wisdom will protect his or her reputation at all costs. The Holy Spirit will only lead us into wisdom and reputable things.

Show that you are full of the Holy Spirit by inclining your heart to wisdom and living above reproach. Your leaders will be encouraged by the standards of your life, and they will look for opportunities to raise you up.

Report + Repetition = Reputation. This equation shows how your reputation is produced from repeated reports from different sources regarding your success or failure and/or your organization's success or failure. How important it is, then, that you clearly define your culture or value system! Unless you want others to make up their minds about your reputation, you must publicize and market the reputation you desire. Make sure that you have a clear and concise culture and value system that you can execute with high efficacy and determination.

CHAPTER FIVE

FORWARD THINKING

Thus says the Lord, the Holy One of Israel, and his Maker: "Ask Me of things to come concerning My sons; and concerning the work of My hands, you command Me (Isaiah 45:11).

THIS IS ONE OF the most important parts of being a leader-servant. It will give the leader you serve so much relief as you stay teachable, pliable, and flexible. Possessing forward thinking will help you be flexible; having a prophetic inclination will give you the heads up on possible transitions ahead. Have you ever ridden tandem on a motorcycle? As a passenger, you must learn to lean into the turn along with the lead rider. If you can't look over the driver's shoulders and foresee when a turn demands a lean, you can throw off the balance of the motorcycle. Just as riding tandem on a motorcycle demands foresight to see and to stay on the motorcycle, working in an organization demands foresight. I have had people say to me, "I knew that you were going to teach that today!" Or "I was just thinking about that!" or "I have been studying that this week." I have also seen some of these people step into arrogance because they could look over my shoulders and see the next turn, but instead of flexing or bending with the turn, they stood straight up and ended up flying off the bike. If God is showing you the next turn, lean into it instead of bragging about seeing it. Your leaning into it is more important than talking about the fact that you see it.

The fact that these people can see the turn is awesome; it means that they have curiosity. Curious people ask a lot of questions. I have a seven-year old, Yosef (who turned seven today), a nine-year old, and a nineteen-month old, who are all very inquisitive. They ask a lot of questions, which can sometimes be hard. Fortunately, it also means that they are thinkers. God says, *"Ask Me of things to come concerning My sons; and concerning the work of My hands"* (Isa. 45:11). There are some things that God won't answer, but two things that He wants us to ask Him about are the future of His children and the Kingdom work. Why would He want us to ask about these things? He wants us to be thinkers. He wants us to be forward thinkers with the same interests: His children and His Kingdom.

God's Interests

Asking a question doesn't irritate God or offend Him; a question to God simply means that you are interested in His answer. It's the subject of our question that interests God. I know what my kids are thinking about by what they ask me. If they ask me about money, then I know that they have been thinking about money. If they ask me about God, then I know that they are thinking about God. Of course, their questions about God are more interesting to me than their questions about money. I get excited when they ask about things that match my interests. We can talk all day about these things if their attention will allow it. I feel that this is how God our Father feels when we approach Him regarding the future of our leaders or His other children. I think that God could talk all day about the works of His hand and His Kingdom, if our attention spans could handle it.

It is our responsibility to keep our attention on the things that excite God. *"You command Me"* has a different meaning from what we would ordinarily think. *Command Me* is the word *tsavah* (tsaw-vaw'): to constitute or enjoin.[1] Once God answers us about the future of His children and the works of His hands, He wants us to join ourselves to the cause. Join the vision; join the force! If God has given you foresight, it is because your curiosity has captured His attention; and now that you see clearly, you have a responsibility to embrace the change and become more flexible than others. Let's go back to the tandem motorcycle analogy: you must lean into the driver and into the turn. Be ready and willing for the changes ahead and prepare your mind and heart to be flexible, so that you won't throw the driver and the bike off balance. After you have seen the vision, don't get flung off the bike because of arrogance—don't close your eyes as the turn comes because of fear. Don't shrink back from a great opportunity to balance out change and keep the momentum of the organization because of fear of what may be around the corner. God would not have given you the foresight and the opportunity if He didn't believe that you could handle it.

The Holy Spirit will work with you according to John 16:13:

> *However, when He, the Spirit of truth, has come, He will guide you into all truth; for He will not speak on His own authority, but whatever He hears He will speak; and He will tell you things to come.*

The Holy Spirit will not only show you the future, but He will guide you into it. Sometimes our future demands things from us that our past has never demanded. This can be intimidating. For this reason, God has sent the Holy Spirit to help us do what we have joined ourselves to. We can count on the Holy Spirit to teach us how to be a dynamic leader-servant man or woman of God. We can count on the Holy Spirit to teach us how to be a dynamic disciple and follower of the vision.

The Holy Spirit will guide, coach, hear, and prophesy in order to keep us fresh servants of the Kingdom of God. We must hear the vision, listen to His words, obey His coaching, and follow His leading. These things will enable us to hear the vision, listen to the words, obey the coaching, and follow the leadership of our leaders. When we join ourselves to God's children and God's work, we also join ourselves to the guidance and direction of the Holy Spirit. Foresight causes us to see the bigger picture, the Kingdom picture. We must not only see the bigger picture, but we must join ourselves to the bigger picture by doing our part, no matter how small or how large.

Endnote

1. "Tsavah"; http://www.studylight.org/lex/heb/view.cgi?number=06680.

PART 2

HEALTHY SOUL

CHAPTER SIX

PROBLEM SOLVERS

There is a man in your kingdom who has the spirit of the holy gods in him. In the time of your father he was found to have insight and intelligence and wisdom like that of the gods. King Nebuchadnezzar your father—your father the king, I say—appointed him chief of the magicians, enchanters, astrologers and diviners. This man Daniel, whom the king called Belteshazzar, was found to have a keen mind and knowledge and understanding, and also the ability to interpret dreams, explain riddles and solve difficult problems. Call for Daniel, and he will tell you what the writing means (Daniel 5:11-12 NIV).

FOR MANY YEARS I believed and taught that every Christian must be filled with the Holy Spirit so that he or she could receive power. In my mind, signs of power were the manifestation of speaking in a heavenly tongue or operating in one of the gifts of the Holy Spirit. After many years of study and frustration, I saw the connection between the Holy Spirit and being filled in a different light. What I saw was that the Holy Spirit doesn't fill us with power only to perform miracles or speak in heavenly languages. He also fills us with sound emotion as in the fruits of the Spirit which are found in the soul. The Holy Spirit doesn't simply give us spiritual abilities, He gives us intellectual and emotional strength. Our background text says that Daniel was a person filled with the Holy Spirit who had insight, intelligence, and wisdom beyond his age. We, like Daniel, can be filled with wisdom, knowledge, counsel, insight, and problem-solving ability, which is also the creativity to invent what has not been.

Insight and Awareness

Insight is something that is highly important to any organization. As a support to your leader, you will have to develop a keen sense of awareness. It's one thing to meet the need of a leader unaware, which means that you did well by accident. It is a whole other story to be able to meet the need of your leader intentionally. It means that you pay attention. One of the most powerful success principles is the principle of awareness—being aware of your surroundings, your leader's needs, your posture, and your timing.

> And the Syrians had gone out by companies, and captured a little girl out of the land of Israel. And she waited on Naaman's wife. And she said to her mistress, I wish my lord were with the prophet in Samaria! For he would recover him from his leprosy. And one went in and told his lord, saying, This and this said the girl from the land of Israel. And the king of Syria said, Go, go in and I will send a letter to the king of Israel. And he departed and took with him ten talents of silver and six thousand of gold, and ten changes of clothing. And he came in with the letter to the king of Israel, saying, And now when this letter has come to you, behold, I have sent Naaman my servant to you (2 Kings 5:2-6 MKJV).

I call this girl a leader-servant. Notice how many people that she influenced by her insight.

Awareness comes from an enlightened mind. When the Holy Spirit gives you insight, He pulls back the covers on things that others may not see, or things that have been right before your eyes. A person cannot repent unless he or she is aware of the need for repentance. A person cannot grow without being made aware of what is possible in the future. Or, as Abraham Maslow famously said, "What is necessary to change a person is to change his awareness of himself."[1] The Holy Spirit will help you understand what you are truly capable of doing. This awareness will be vital to you as a laborer or leader in the Kingdom of God. You must be able to see what others cannot see and use it to increase the Kingdom of God. The rulers of the world called on Daniel because they needed someone to tell them what they couldn't understand. A problem is simply a solution that hasn't been seen yet.

Awareness also comes from something that we have talked about already: intellectual curiosity and asking the right questions. Intellectual curiosity causes you to ask probing questions that demand a specific answer. Learn to ask questions of yourself and others which demand an extensive response. Don't ask questions that will allow you or others to answer with a single word; after doing this for some time, you will develop the power to see without questions. When a team can develop this type of awareness, there will be such a flow of success and increase that all who see it will be amazed. As a leader, I love when someone is so aware that they know my needs before I ask or even announce the need. This awareness anticipates the possibilities from all angles.

Not only are problem solvers people of awareness, but they are also lifetime learners. The Holy Spirit has filled us for the purpose of changing our minds. God's Spirit anoints or rests upon us for exploits, and we are filled with the Spirit for intelligence. The Book of Daniel says that Daniel was filled with God's Spirit, giving him *"a keen mind and knowledge and understanding, and also the ability to interpret dreams, explain riddles and solve difficult problems"* (Dan. 5:12 NIV).

The power of a keen mind, knowledge, and understanding helps us to imagine the unbelievable and invent solutions for problems. Daniel's ability to interpret dreams, explain riddles, and solve difficult problems has also been delivered to us, because it is all found in the same Holy Spirit.

Becoming a Problem Solver

How does it all work? Problem solving involves possibility thinking, deeper intellectual curiosity of how things work, and confidence that you can make a difference. If you don't have the confidence that you can make a change in the circumstances, then a solution will never be revealed to you. If you believe that you live a guided life and that the Holy Spirit will reveal to you the way to make that change possible, then all things will be possible. The best way to operate as a problem solver is to gather as many facts as possible about the pending issue, place all of the issues on the table, invite the Holy Spirit to sit at the table with you, and begin asking questions. Let your questions go all over the place. Get accustomed to asking questions that demand a longer answer or investigation. Each question should bring to your attention a greater awareness of your problem and its needs. Again, the more you know about it, the sooner your answer will come. Sometimes the first level of questions is simply fact finding and not necessarily problem solving. If your questions don't lead you down a road of research, then you need to ask better questions.

Rabbit trails in asking questions really are valuable; you never know when you are going to actually find a rabbit hole with answers. Your rabbit run may also lead you down a train of thought that you can use later for a different issue. You can do this in a group setting, but a group setting doesn't necessarily guarantee problem solving. We take an approach at our problem solving and creative meetings that is used by many advertising agencies, where the creative flow is allowed to happen in a meeting and creative juices are not stifled. In the book *Bang!*, Linda Kaplin Thaler talks about how she allowed her creative group to go on rabbit trails in their creative meetings because one never knows what new idea will come out of it. The AFLAC duck ad campaign came out of one of those rabbit trails, raising the company's profile from zero to being instantly recognizable. This idea came while one of the "creatives" went on a seemingly irrelevant rabbit trail, saying the name AFLAC with a strange voice because they had hit a creative wall. Linda mentions in the book that she encourages this strategy in such creative meetings all the time. Just about everyone knows about the AFLAC duck because of this creative freedom. Allowing a little freedom to enter into your next planning, business, or creative meeting may solve your next big problem. After all, creativity is the only way to solve problems.

Problem solvers love a challenge, problem solvers are bottom-line oriented, and problem solvers are creative innovators. Problem solving is a mind-set, a mind-set of "whatever it takes," and "I'll never give up until I reach my goals."

If you know that you have unlimited wisdom in your corner, you will approach things differently. The Bible says,

> *If any of you lacks wisdom, let him ask of God, who gives to all liberally and without reproach, and it will be given to him. But let him ask in faith, with no doubting* (James 1:5-6).

Let me put it this way: suppose that every time you needed wisdom or knowledge, you could call the wisest person on earth to ask any question you could think of. Now, supposing this wise person would give you the correct answer every time, how often would you take advantage of this? Weekly, if not daily? This is a picture of our relationship with the Holy Spirit. He is the wisest person on earth, and we have the ability to contact

Him and ask Him anything, to be empowered with absolute intelligence.

One of the biggest neglects of the Body of Christ is the fact that we have seen God as power, as feeling, as forgiving, but not as the greatest intellectual mind ever. If God were the greatest mind on earth, how would you approach Him? Let me show you how God wants to relate with you. We find it in Isaiah 11:2, which says, *"The Spirit of the Lord will rest on Him—the Spirit of wisdom and of understanding, the Spirit of counsel and of power, the Spirit of knowledge and of the fear of the Lord"* (NIV).

The Spirit of the Lord rests upon us to increase our intellectual capacity. He gives wisdom and understanding, counsel and the ability to counsel, the power to acquire knowledge, and the fear of the Lord. Even the fear of the Lord deals with your mind, for it is the beginning of wisdom and the hatred of evil; actually, it is a choice to love righteousness. These things affect your intellect. God is intellectual, and He created us to be intellectually stimulated and productive. Our problems are not to stump us, but to inspire us intellectually to find a solution, not only for ourselves, but for all whom we serve and minister.

It is a great thing to be able to solve problems whenever the need arises; it is an exceptional thing to be able to foresee a problem and to develop a preventative solution. This ability is available to you and me, 24/7, as we build a closer relationship with the wisest Person on earth! Your leader will be able to rest in the fact that you are not only in the game, but also intellectually ahead of the game and in charge. Your leader will appreciate your problem-solving skills and will call upon you in times of need. But you must assure your leader that you have his heart if you truly want him to trust in what you have to say.

Endnote

1. See http://www.abraham-maslow.com/m_motivation/Maslow_Quotes. asp.

CHAPTER SEVEN

AN ARMOR BEARER MENTALITY

NOT EVERYONE SERVING A leader is an armor bearer, but every person serving should have an armor bearer's mind-set. In biblical times, an *armor bearer* (Hebrew *nasa' keli*, "one carrying weapons") was a person selected by prominent officers to bear their armor, to stand by them in danger, and to carry out their orders, somewhat as adjutants in modern service.[1] I believe that the closer you are to the leader, the more of this mind-set you should possess. I don't want to go into the structure of an organization, but I do want to say that if you are close to the leader, you should work hard on developing these skills. You must possess the mind-set of an armor bearer whether you are a first, second, or third-line leader. Earlier, in the introduction to this book, I talked about drivers, developers, and detailers. I call the driver the first-level leader, the developer the second-level leader, and the detailer the third-level leader. These levels are not based upon their importance, but are based upon how closely they work with the visionary, whom I call the director.

There are some very important lessons to learn from the Bible regarding this mind-set. Let's start with First Samuel 14. Your leader needs you to connect with his heart and passion so that he can feel your loyalty and can freely lead you into the next level of your life and ministry.

> *Jonathan said to his young armor-bearer, "Come, let's go over to the outpost of those uncircumcised fellows. Perhaps the Lord will act in our behalf. Nothing can hinder the Lord from saving, whether by many or by few." "Do all that you have in mind," his armor-bearer said. "Go ahead; I am with you heart and soul." Jonathan said, "Come, then; we will cross over toward the men and let them see us. If they say to us, 'Wait there until we come to you,' we will stay where we are and not go up to them. But if they say, 'Come up to us,' we will climb up, because that will be our sign that the Lord has given them into our hands." So both of them showed themselves to the Philistine outpost. "Look!" said the Philistines. "The Hebrews are crawling out of the holes they were hiding in." The men of the outpost shouted to Jonathan and his armor-bearer, "Come up to us and we'll teach you a lesson." So Jonathan said to his armor-bearer, "Climb up after me; the Lord has given them into the hand of Israel." Jonathan climbed up, using his hands and feet, with his armor-bearer right behind him. The Philistines fell before Jonathan, and his armor-bearer followed and killed behind him. In that first attack Jonathan and his armor-bearer killed some twenty men in an area of about half an acre. Then panic struck the whole army—those in the camp and field, and those in the outposts and raiding parties—and the ground shook. It was a panic sent by God* (1 Samuel 14:6-15 NIV).

This is such a great story to study regarding the mind-set of an armor bearer. Let's start with verse 6, specifically: "*Come, let's go over to the outpost of those uncircumcised fellows.*" We can ascertain a few things from this statement. First, the armor bearer was available and accessible. Your leader will need you to have this same mind-set. I have had many people come to me with an apparent heart to serve; they say things like, "I am here for you," or "I am committed to you," but when I call on them, they seem to have excuses for why they can't help. After a few times, I simply stop asking. Your leader will need to know that he or she can count on you when it is time to go to war.

Secondly, I see in Jonathan a leader who knew his armor bearer was trustworthy enough to go into battle with. Your leader must feel that he can trust you. Your leader should never feel naked or uncovered; he should always feel that someone has his back.

Thirdly, Jonathan obviously enjoyed being around the armor bearer. In order for this to be so, his armor bearer could never allow familiarity to enter into the relationship. Let me give you a few examples of what familiarity looks like in a leader and follower relationship.

There are some key words in the next two passages that give away a mind-set of familiarity. The first scenario is a warning for family and friends who serve a leader who has been raised up in your midst. Because you may know them better than anyone else, it might be a very hard thing to see a friend or family member excel into leadership and at the same time maintain respect for their authority.

> *And Miriam and Aaron spake against Moses because of the Ethiopian woman whom he had married: for he had married an Ethiopian woman. And they said, Hath the Lord indeed spoken only by Moses? hath he not spoken also by us? And the Lord heard it* (Numbers 12:1-2).

Miriam was the one who took care of Moses, and Aaron was a very close brother, if not his best friend. This wrong mind-set has its own vocabulary: "*And they said, Hath the Lord indeed spoken only by Moses? hath he not spoken also by us?"* This form of thinking is dangerous not only to the leaders whom they follow and their organization but it also endangers themselves. As we take note of this passage, a very important statement must be recognized: *"And the Lord heard it."* They were boasting about their ability to hear God when God heard them. Read the whole story for yourself in the Scripture to see the outcome of what happens to those who defy the leaders whom God has positioned. It's not pretty.

The next example that I want to give we call the Sin of Korah and is also from Moses' life as a leader. The language is still the same for this mind-set of familiarity. The strange thing is that all of these people witnessed the rebellion of Miriam and didn't learn. Sometimes people will not learn from simply watching.

> *Now Korah, the son of Izhar, the son of Kohath, the son of Levi, with Dathan and Abiram, the sons of Eliab, and On, the son of Peleth, sons of Reuben, took men: and they rose up before Moses, with certain of the children of Israel, two hundred and fifty princes of the congregation, called to the assembly, men of renown; and they assembled themselves together against Moses and against Aaron, and said unto them, Ye take too much upon you, seeing all the congregation are holy, every one of them, and Jehovah is among them: wherefore then lift ye up yourselves above the assembly of Jehovah? And when Moses heard it, he fell upon his face: and he spake unto Korah and unto all his company, saying, In the morning Jehovah will show who are his, and who is holy, and will cause him to come near unto him: even him whom he shall choose will he cause to come near unto him. This do: take you censers, Korah, and all his company; and put fire in them, and put incense upon them before Jehovah to-morrow: and it shall be that the man whom Jehovah doth choose, he shall be holy: ye take too much upon you, ye sons of Levi"* (Numbers 16:1-6 MKJV).

The leaders who followed Moses got too big for their britches. Self-righteousness will breed contempt and familiarity. Avoid self-righteousness by pursuing humility. A great leader is not great because of charisma or some outward display. Moses was a meek man, but because he had been through this before, he stood his ground with these arrogant followers. Even meek leaders can stand their ground when protecting a position given by God. Sometimes people misunderstand meekness and think that it is weakness. Self-righteous people will always try to place themselves on the same level or above the leader through faultfinding and pointing out what seems like a flaw or weakness.

At times I have had people purposefully avoid addressing me by my title of *Pastor*, simply to make the point that they don't need to respect me. This has always been to their detriment and never mine.

The leader should never feel that the armor bearer has forgotten who she is, or about the mandate or the mantle on her life. The armor bearer should know how to separate the times and the seasons. When it is time to bear armor, it is not the time to get private ministry. Private ministry happens in the camp, not on the field. Stay in rank and fulfill your duty; your leader will not forget your diligence.

Let's move on to the next part of First Samuel 14: 6 NIV "*Perhaps the Lord will act in our behalf. Nothing can hinder the Lord from saving, whether by many or by few.*"Jonathan was comfortable enough with his armor bearer to share his plan of God's deliverance even though it seemed far fetched and near to impossible. We can see by the answer of the armor bearer why Jonathan would feel comfortable: "*Do all that you have in mind,*" his armor-bearer said. "*Go ahead; I am with you heart and soul.*" The armor bearer had to possess the same convictions as his leader; he had to have the same readiness, willingness, and faith. The Philistines had to become not only the enemies of his leader, but his personal enemies. Jonathan had to trust that his armor bearer believed in him before he could let his armor bearer know the details of the plan. Sometimes your leader will need for you to trust in *her*, rather than her *plan*.

Trusting Your Leader

My wife and I had dinner with a couple that had weathered some storms with us, and all they had to say was, "We believe in you both and believe that you hear from God." They were trusting that we live surrendered lives before God. It is easy to find a leader with a plan; it is harder to find a leader who relies on God. Rely on God and believe in your leader who relies on God, and you will never go wrong. My wife and I have used this saying: "They bet on the wrong horse." We use it for people who rely on plans instead of on the guidance of the Lord. So what if the plan is not complete? We see only in part. Never judge your leader for not having the whole picture. Jesus didn't have the whole picture; He simply had His relationship with the Father and lived a surrendered and obedient life to God. Give your leader a chance to surrender to and obey the Lord; it's not always going to make sense. God's plans most often go through modifications—a great example of this is the ram in the bush God provided for Abraham after testing him— nevertheless, your heart of surrender should never change.

A leader who only sees a part of the big picture or overall plan must become a seeker of wisdom through prayer and wise counsel. A good armor bearer understands that sometimes a leader will first need to know that you are with her before she can reveal to you the whole scoop. Not everyone can handle this, but everyone who is close to the leader will need to develop this mind-set. Leaders need *true* "yes men"—those who will believe first and then look for ways to make it come to pass. Leaders need people who can be both optimistic and detail-oriented enough to ask the developmental questions.

Are You With Me?

The next thing that we must take note of is that the armor bearer relayed his position on the matter up front. He didn't gripe, complain, or question; he said, *"I am with you heart and soul."* A leader is always asking the question, "Are they with me?" Why? Because if he is not being followed, he is not leading. A leader is always looking for people who are with him. Leaders need to know that the people following have spent time mentally evaluating their commitment, have counted the price of following the leader beforehand, and have meditated on all the possibilities of serving this leader. Jonathan's attendant didn't have to stop and think about the situation, because his heart and soul were already knit to his leader. A leader needs to have the confidence that he will not have to look back to see if the people who started with him are still there. Your heart must be given to your leader, and you must be emotionally connected in order to be an armor bearer. To be a dynamic armor bearer, you must be mentally and emotionally engaged with your leader's vision and dreams; this is the first stage of developing the soul of service. One of the best examples of this kind of armor bearer is seen in a movie called "Thirteen Days." In this movie, presidential aide Kenneth P. O'Donnell (Kevin Costner) and President John F. Kennedy (Bruce Greenwood) along with his closest advisors try to find the best way to end a potentially devastating showdown with the U.S.S.R. in October 1962. Kenneth P. O'Donnell was a supportive believer in the President whom he served. He stood by him as these tough choices needed to be made, and never questioned his authority in the presence of other subordinates. Behind closed doors, he was a friend who never overstepped his boundaries, but had the freedom to tell the truth about what he felt and perceived. This picture of the presidential aide is an easy analogy to pull from, but we can see this same relationship between a CEO and the vice-president who is to execute the dreams and desire of the CEO with nothing more than a simple directive. Likewise, the head coach of an athletic team must bring to pass the vision of the team's owner.

In the book *God's Armor Bearer*, Terry Nance illustrates what he calls a faithful armor bearer:

Some time ago my pastor, Happy Caldwell of Agape Church in Little Rock, Arkansas, met with the Billy Graham Crusade team which was planning a series of meetings in our city. The crusade coordinator started his talk by stating that he had been with Billy Graham the least amount of time of any of the ministers on the staff. "I have only been with Billy for 23 years."

Billy Graham was not in the meeting. His armor bearers were conducting the meeting and this armor bearer had *only* been with Billy Graham for 23 years. As I read this, I realized that even though Billy Graham is a hero, he would not be able to do what he did without armor bearers who believed in him and his mission, staying with him for a minimum of 23 years. I would daresay that an armor bearer needs to have spent some time with the leader in order to really own the vision. I don't think that two years will do it; you haven't even overcome any great obstacles within a two-year time period. Gaining the heart of your leader takes time.

Tactfulness

Jonathan's helper chose his words carefully. My wife always says, "Our words are weighty; they carry great force or power. We need to be careful of what we say." Your words are weighty. If you have this understanding, you will guard your words. David said, *"Help me, Lord, to keep my mouth shut and my lips sealed"* (see Ps. 141:3). An armor bearer should know when to speak and when to be quiet. Tactfulness is a characteristic of a good armor bearer. We opened this book with an armor bearer who was judged by the prophet because he didn't know when to stay quiet. He died an early death, and the king could no longer lean on him. Your own words will make or break your ministry to your leader.

Taking Risks

In addition, the armor bearer in First Samuel 14 was a risk taker. I believe that it takes a special breed of person to be on the ground floor of something. Whether it's planting a church, starting a business, or going to war, the beachhead needs roughnecks to take it. In business, these are entrepreneurs; entrepreneurs love the building of the company more than the running of it. Managers love the running of the organization more than the expansion; and technicians love the detailed, artistic dynamics of the company. In the early stages of any organization, everybody needs to have an entrepreneurial mind-set inclined toward taking risks. Jonathan needed a risk taker, not a manager or a technician. Later, the armor bearer could return to thinking like a technician or a manager. At the inception, we need to fight for the life of the vision and organization.

Following the Plan

Once Jonathan had support from his armor bearer, the plan unfolded:

> *Come, then; we will cross over toward the men and let them see us. If they say to us, 'Wait there until we come to you,' we will stay where we are and not go up to them. But if they say, 'Come up to us,' we will climb up, because that will be our sign that the Lord has given them into our hands.* (1 Samuel 14:8-10 NIV)

So many people get lost right here. This is where the *"I am with you heart and soul"* must stand up—after you hear the "crazy" plan of the leader. You can't turn back if you don't like the plan: "He said that we were going to do this," or "He said that we were going to do that." Sometimes the plan must be modified. You might not agree with the change, but you must still stay fully submitted. Submission calls for you to follow the plan.

The only exception is if what you are called on to do breaks God's law and/or man's law. Let God and time be the judge.

The Bible goes on to say, *"So both of them showed themselves."* Again, the armor bearer had enough confidence in his leader to go on with the plan, no matter how strange it sounded to him, even to the point of humiliation:

> *'Look!' said the Philistines. 'The Hebrews are crawling out of the holes they were hiding in.' The men of the outpost shouted to Jonathan and his armor-bearer, 'Come up to us and we'll teach you a lesson. So Jonathan said to his armor-bearer, 'Climb up after me; the Lord has given them into the hand of Israel.' Jonathan climbed up, using his hands and feet, with his armor-bearer right behind him* (1 Samuel 14:11-13 NIV).

Stay Humble

Humility means surrendering your strength and gifts to serve a bigger plan. Jesus humbled Himself to serve God the Father. Jesus had the right to change the plan by calling forth angels, but He was on earth on an assignment from the Father to save all humankind, not to save Himself. Jonathan's armor bearer was willing to charge his enemy alongside his leader as they climbed into the enemy's camp. The armor bearer was willing to go the extra mile. He didn't stop at the bottom and say, "This goes beyond my armor bearer job description." Humility will go the extra mile, the soul of service will go the extra mile, and God's armor bearer will go the extra mile. With helpers like Jonathan's armor bearer, any leader will be able to achieve the vision and mandates on their life, ministry, or business. The report of the great deeds of these servants will be shouted in the camp:

> *Jonathan climbed up, using his hands and feet, with his armor-bearer right behind him. The Philistines fell before*

*Jonathan, and his armor-bearer followed and killed behind
him. In that first attack Jonathan and his armor-bearer
killed some twenty men in an area of about half an acre.
Then panic struck the whole army—those in the camp and
field, and those in the outposts and raiding parties—and
the ground shook. It was a panic sent by God.* (1 Samuel
14:13-15 TNIV)

Jonathan wasn't the only victor listed; the armor bearer was listed
throughout the whole story. The leader and the armor bearer will share in
the praise and in the rewards of their labor.

Ministry of Peace and Comfort

First Samuel 16:21-23 also has a good lesson to be learned regarding
the mind-set of the armor bearer:

*David came to Saul and entered his service. Saul liked him
very much, and David became one of his armor-bearers.
Then Saul sent word to Jesse, saying, "Allow David to
remain in my service, for I am pleased with him." Whenever
the spirit from God came upon Saul, David would take his
harp and play. Then relief would come to Saul; he would
feel better, and the evil spirit would leave him* (NIV).

In this Scripture text we see that the armor bearer should be liked by
the leader, and the leader should be pleased with his service. The gifts and
talents you display should comfort your leader. Your leader should not have
to tolerate the service that you perform, but should be ministered to from
your gift. As David brought peace and calm to Saul, so should your gift and
talent bring peace and calm to your leader.

Faithful and Trustworthy

My final thoughts on the mind-set of the armor bearer come from Acts 10:4-8:

> So he said to him, "Your prayers and your alms have come up for a memorial before God. Now send men to Joppa, and send for Simon whose surname is Peter. He is lodging with Simon, a tanner, whose house is by the sea. He will tell you what you must do." And when the angel who spoke to him had departed, Cornelius called two of his household servants and a devout soldier from among those who waited on him continually. So when he had explained all these things to them, he sent them to Joppa.

Your leader should be able to send you on a divinely-appointed assignment knowing that you will get the job done. Cornelius was able to call two of his servants and a devout soldier from those who were continually serving him, which means that he had seen their faithfulness. Divine assignments are distributed to people who have proven to be faithful. Whether you believe that you are a future leader or whether you are a lifetime server, God looks to bless those who have a proven track record in serving someone else's vision and mandates.

> Whoever can be trusted with very little can also be trusted with much, and whoever is dishonest with very little will also be dishonest with much. So if you have not been trustworthy in handling worldly wealth, who will trust you with true riches? And if you have not been trustworthy with someone else's property, who will give you property of your own? (Luke 16:10-12 NIV)

Promotion comes from being a faithful and trustworthy servant. Master the skills and mind-set of an armor bearer even if that is not your official position, and you will find the grace and favor of God on your life to achieve great things.

Endnote

1. "Nasa"; http://www.studylight.org/lex/heb/view.cgi?number=05375; "Keli"; http://www.studylight.org/lex/heb/view.cgi?number=03627; Merrill F. Unger, *The New Unger's Bible Dictionary* (Chicago: Moody Publishers, 2006).

Chapter Eight

FEEDING AND STARVING

So I say, let the Holy Spirit guide your lives. Then you won't be doing what your sinful nature craves. The sinful nature loves to do evil, which is just opposite of what the Spirit wants. And the Spirit gives us desires that are opposite from what the sinful nature desires. These two forces are constantly fighting each other, so you are not free to carry out your good intentions. But when you are directed by the Spirit, you are not under obligation to the law of Moses (Galatians 5:16-18 NLT).

LIFE IS ABOUT FEEDING and starving. Whatever you feed lives, and whatever you starve dies. If you feed negativity, you will be negative. If you want to stay positive, you will need to starve negativity and feed positivity. Feeding and starving are choices and come with forethought and preparation. It's the typical cause and effect, which is a simple formula: every effect has a cause. If we learn to control the cause so that we can obtain the desired effect, then we will be able to live our dreams. Vision is not a cause nor is it an effect. A cause is action, and an effect is the result of the action. Changing your actions will produce a change in your results. It is like simple economics. Economics is the study of cause and effect. Economics is the process of predicting the flow of a currency or commodity and the cause of the flow of that currency or commodity through measurements. Sometimes we have to do an economic analysis of our love lives, family lives, health, serving, or ministry.

Economics is not just about the effect but also about the cause. Analyze all of the results and what feeding produced that result. After you realize what you have been feeding to produce unwanted fruit, then you can figure out what you do desire and start the necessary actions to produce that desired end. For example, if you don't like your *love handles,* then you should starve the cravings of going to the fridge at 11:00 P.M. to eat a tub of ice cream. The cause: going to the fridge and eating a tub of ice cream. The effect: 20 unwanted pounds. So the action becomes feeding the right emotions and starving the wrong emotions. Our emotions control our cravings, our cravings control our actions, and our focus controls our emotions. Focusing on the craving allows my emotions to produce the result by default; yet focusing on the desired result will help take charge of my emotions. This allows me to control my cravings and my actions, which in turn will produce my desired result. Romans 13:14 says, *"But put on the Lord Jesus Christ, and make no provision for the flesh, to fulfill its lusts."* Make no provision for the human nature with its frailties, physical or moral, and its passions.

Destructive Patterns

Destructive emotions and cravings need to be addressed. According to Romans 8:12-14, continuing in destructive patterns will bring forth death:

> *Therefore, dear brothers and sisters, you have no obligation*
> *to do what your sinful nature urges you to do. For if you live*

by its dictates, you will die. But if through the power of the Holy Spirit you put to death the deeds of your sinful nature, you will live. For all who are led by the Spirit of God are children of God (NLT).

The Bible says that God's desire is that none should perish, but if following your natural urges brings death, then living a submitted, Spirit-led, Christian character-based life will bring life. The power of the Holy Spirit enters your life through your personal submission to the life that God has determined. The Holy Spirit desires to lead you into the life specifically designed for you. Your *natural man* has a craving for things that do not please God, and it wars directly against what the Holy Spirit wants to accomplish in and through you. Your *spirit man* seeks only to please God; this is your spirit's essence of life.

We must actively and thoughtfully subdue our passions; you and I must keep our emotions under control. From pride to laziness to lust, I have had to get my emotions under control many times. The one emotion most dangerous to my destiny was fear of failure. I had no problem dreaming of great things; the hard part was getting moving. I would make a new excuse every day as to why I couldn't start working on my dream. Finally, I got fed up with simply dreaming. I wanted to achieve something in life. I initially started pursuing my dream by helping someone else achieve his. This approach, working with others to achieve their dreams, allowed me to see that what we dream can actually come true.

The other thing that I did and still do to overcome the fear of failure is ask the following question: "What would I do if I were not afraid?" Once I realize what I would do if I were not afraid, I then choose to do it. "Do it afraid" has become a statement that we use in our organization a lot. We do not allow fear to be an excuse for not moving forward. We must live by the Holy Spirit and be led by the Holy Spirit in every part of our lives. Our spouses, as well as our co-workers, should feel the effects of our determination to be spiritual and Spirit led. There cannot be any area in our lives where we tolerate anything but the best that God has for us. That is what He desires to lead us into—the best! Galatians 5:24-25 is very clear about what God expects from us:

> *Those who belong to Christ Jesus have nailed the passions and desires of their sinful nature to His cross and crucified them there. Since we are living now by the Spirit, let us follow the Spirit's leading in every part of our lives* (NLT).

You must learn to master your emotions through feeding and starving. Remember, whatever you feed lives, grows, and thrives. Whatever you starve dies. If the natural man is fed, it will live, and you will naturally starve your spirit man. If you feed your spirit man, your natural man will die. Below, I will exemplify some emotions and actions of emotion which cause destruction.

- The animal nature is based upon primal instinct: what feels good, looks good, and tastes good. A dog has no reasoning power; it lives based upon a set of instincts. God has given us the power of choice. We have a moral obligation to live intentionally, instead of by what feels good. Revenge may gratify me, but it will not help me live a more contented life. Starve the animal nature and feed self-control.

- Gossip keeps account of wrongs. If you find yourself gossiping, you must realize that you are not only sinning against God and the person you are talking about, but you are also drawing into sin the person that you are talking to. Furthermore, you are sinning by hating your brother or sister; love is not in your heart. Avoid gossip with a passion, for it is a destructive force in the lives of the wicked. If you desire life, it is found in the lives of those who have love in their hearts. Love covers, and hates attacks; therefore, starve gossip and feed love. Love overlooks all faults.

❧ Fear is a product of improper focus. The difference between faith and fear is a heartbeat. If you truly think about it, you will understand that fear and excitement run on the same nervous system. If you can change your focus to something that is exciting, your nervous system won't skip a beat. When you are afraid, stop looking at what is creating the fearfulness, unless you are faced with danger. Fear is the beginning of your fight or flight reflex; under dangerous circumstances, fear releases adrenalin to aid in escaping or in accomplishing victory. Some fear brings wisdom as your nerves respond to dangerous situations; some fear brings stress and paralysis. If you find yourself paralyzed by fear, focus on something that will bring you hope, joy, and peace. Sometimes my son will wake up from a bad dream; we briefly talk about the dream, then we refocus him on something else that brings him joy. For him, it is a trip to Disneyland. We focus on what he would do, who he would see, and what he would eat at the park. After a few minutes, the bad dream is totally removed from his mind. Mickey, Goofy, and friends are dancing through his brain, while his emotions have transformed from fear to excitement. For him it is Disneyland; for me it is my future; for you it may be your past. Whatever it is, use it. Fool your nerves by changing your focus.

Starve fear and feed vision.

♦ Doubt is a paralyzing poison to your faith. Starve doubts; feed faith. When I speak of feeding faith, I mean putting action to your vision. You can confess, proclaim, or prophecy, but none of these things will manifest without your action. Action is the only thing that can give you results in your life, your marriage, your business, and your ministry. Doubt produces an action: the action of procrastination, the action of deciding to do nothing, and the action of doing everything opposite to what you should be doing. Faith takes action toward your vision and dream. Faith takes action even if you are afraid. Do it scared; take the action while frightened out of your wits, and you will still produce the results, which will eventually produce confidence.

♦ Selfish ambition is the opposite of Christ-likeness and of servanthood. Ambition alone is not bad; it is defined by the desired result of the ambition. If you are the only benefactor of the ambition, then the ambition is selfish, self-serving, self-gratifying, self-glorifying, and self-instituted. In order to starve selfish ambition, there must be a change in focus from getting to giving. A person like Mother Teresa or Billy Graham can have an ambitious pursuit that benefits others. I think we all would agree that these two individuals were ambitious in their achievements; they were driven to achieve in these realms. If you can connect the ambition that is in your heart with a need in someone else's life, you will live a rewarding and ambitious life.

This will, in actuality, give you what you personally desired in the first place. Solomon asked for wisdom and understanding so that he could properly serve the people, and he received both of those things along with riches, honor, and long life. If you seek what is right, God will give to you all of the other things that pertain to life and godliness. Discover and develop the soul of service; serve with your heart, thoughts, feelings, and intentions, You will be blessed to be a blessing to others. Starve selfish ambition and feed servanthood. This is the Kingdom way.

❀ Insecurity keeps you from being the real you. Insecure people live with masks on; their mask may manifest in anger, pride, or isolation. Insecure people deal with fear and shame—the companions of not wanting to be found out or seem vulnerable. Combat insecurity with the development of a healthy God-confidence and personal confidence. When I say confidence, I mean a security in the fact that you are created in God's image and that He is perfecting you each and every day. With the understanding that you are changing every day into the image of God, you will find relief in not having to be perfect now. Insecure people don't want anyone to see what is really going on in their lives, so they have sharp tongues and strange attitudes all to disguise the fact that there is hurt in the heart and a struggle in the mind. First, there must be recognition that you are not broken, but growing. There is a big difference between being broken and simply growing. One sees God as a mechanic; the other sees God as a farmer. Seeing God as a cultivator allows us to gain confidence that He has planted a particular crop and will fight the birds and shelter it from the storm to see that crop spring forth and be harvested. The farmer doesn't give up on his crop unless it ceases to live. Insecurity is an internal death, yet confidence trusts that something new and fresh will spring forth. I can be confident that I will be strengthened tomorrow. Secondly, you must get a different picture of who you desire to be. If you change the way you see yourself, others will also see you differently. The giants saw that the children of Israel saw themselves as grasshoppers, so that's how they saw the children of Israel (see Num. 13:31-33). Confident people can outlast the storms of criticism and life's unfair ways in order to reach their ultimate life. Could you see Jesus pretending like He was not being crucified while He was being dragged off and beaten to a pulp? No, He confidently said, "This is my cup." In order for Him to be who He was meant to become, He had to drink this cup and step into greatness. Be confident that there is greatness inside of you, and you will overcome any thoughts of what people think of you, which is the root of all insecurity. Starve insecurity and feed confidence.

❧ Shame is an interesting emotion; living without shame is virtually impossible unless your conscience has been totally seared. We must maintain at least a small amount of shame for the sake of discretion. A small amount of shame is like an inoculation against shameful acts. It is because of this small amount of shame that we act or dress modestly. We don't usually call it shame. We actually call it modesty. But when a person doesn't have any modesty, we say, "Don't you have any shame?" The kind of shame that we must starve is the type that tells us that we are defective because of something that we have done or something that has been done to us. Shame wants to keep these things hidden from the sight of others. In order to break shame, you must develop a covenant relationship in Heaven and on earth. Covenant relationships allow you to be vulnerable with someone who will not judge you or condemn you. This allows you to be able to process the pain and overcome the shame. I have a covenant relationship with God, with my wife, my pastor, and a few friends (in that order) who keep me accountable and vulnerable. Discretion is healthy; shame is the product of a low self-image, which perpetuates more shameful (and shameless) acts. God is the healer of the brokenhearted and the less than perfect. Be vulnerable to God first, and He will enable you to be soft and vulnerable once again. You are not Humpty Dumpty; God or the King can put you back together again! Starve shame and feed vulnerability.

❦ Anger never has, nor ever will produce God's intentions. One day as I was on my way home, I was disturbed by something that had happened at the office. My wife was misunderstood or misrepresented by someone at the office, and it created a small problem, but the problem really irritated me. On the way home, I was thinking of how I would bring the subject up to my wife. As I went to put my key in the door to open it, the Holy Spirit asked me one simple question, which was, "Is this going to bring peace into your house?" I immediately stopped in my tracks. The Holy Spirit gave me an opportunity to make a choice. What is more important: making a point or feeding peace in my home? Of course feeding the peace in my home is more important. It was definitely most important to God, so I didn't say anything. A few days later, the truth came forth, and I would have had to apologize to my wife for a foolish act and for falling into the trap. You feed anger through the focus you have, and you feed peace through the focus you have. If I focus on the problem, then I will only get more angry; if I change the focus to keeping the peace, then anger leaves, and my mind starts to think of ways to keep the peace. So I have continued asking myself the question, "Will this bring peace?" The Bible says to do everything that we can to live in peace as far as it is up to us (see Eph. 4:3; Heb. 12:14). Will this bring peace? I have noticed that the only thing that brings increase is peace and unity. Anger destroys unity and decreases everything in its way; conversely, wherever peace is, unity can be found. Remember that if you desire increase, you must first desire peace. As you feed peace, you will also bring forth increase. Starve anger and feed peace.

❧ There are several things that make complaining possible. One is the "grass is greener on the other side" mentality. The grass on the other side is actually the same grass. Usually after spending a few days on the other side, the complainer realizes that it is the same field, the same grass, and the same irritations. The problem is not the grass, but the one looking at the grass. The Bible says that the children of Israel came to a place called Marah as they were walking in the wilderness. When they came to the water brook at Marah, they found it to be bitter (see Exod. 15:22-24). I have read a study of this Scripture written by a rabbi. The rabbi says that his understanding of this story was that the people's hearts were bitter, which, in turn, affected their taste. They complained at Marah. I believe that bitterness is the principal mind-set that causes complaining. A person prone to complaining has a heart issue; it's an adopted attitude. In order to destroy this attitude, we must learn to rejoice at all times and through all circumstances. If not, we will believe that the world must be fair and that we are always getting the short end of the stick. Joy is an internal decision. Joy doesn't come from other people; joy comes from a shift in perspective and attitude. Cultivate joy in your heart through thinking on things that are praiseworthy. These things can be from the past, the present, or the hope of the future. Another great way of keeping your heart clean from complaining is to keep a victory journal where you log at least one victory for each day. My wife and I keep a whiteboard in our garage, and we bring it into our living room during confusing or discouraging times. On this board we look at the options, remember God's promises, and write out possible plans. Whatever system you use, use it consistently to cultivate the right attitude so that you can avoid bitterness in the heart and ultimately avoid complaining in the mind and mouth. Starve complaining and feed joy.

❧ Feeling sorry for yourself is so dangerous. Self-pity demands that you get attention from being depressed or confused. Self-pity only exists in the presence of others. When a person who shows signs of self-pity in public is alone, this self-pity can actually become depression. I have read in an article in *Psychology Today*, "What Causes Depression?", that one of many ways that depression can start is from self-pity. Depression is dangerous; if a depressed person doesn't find help, he or she will ultimately self-destruct. Self-pity is the cry for help from a needy person. Neediness will drive this person to get attention in any way possible; he or she simply wants to be loved or encouraged. Yet that rarely ever helps, for it will only feed the neediness. Neediness is like a black hole; you throw things into it, and they never return. People who struggle with self-pity and depression have become inwardly focused; it greatly helps to combat these emotions with compassion and the gift of mercy. I know this to be true because it was the way I overcame self-pity, which eventually turned into depression. The Lord prompted me to go minister at the convalescent home to those who were in a greater need than I was. There are many ways to overcome depression. The most important thing is that anyone dealing with these emotions takes charge of their life so that things don't get worse. Once they do, they will find their meaning in life through helping others. They will be able to mend many hurting hearts because they know what it feels like to need someone. These people are looking for meaning and significance; simply put, they will find all these things through compassionate acts for others. This will break the cycle, but they will still need to develop their God-confidence. The danger with becoming overly helpful is that it could become another way to fulfill neediness. Starve self-pity and feed compassion.

Arrogance and pride are cousins, but they are different. Arrogance exalts its talents and gifts beyond measure because of insecurity and pride. Pride pretends to have certain gifts and talents which are not possessed because of the same insecurity. Luke 14:8-10 gives us the instruction not to take the best seat lest we are embarrassed when we are asked to sit in a less important place. Satan's insecurity allowed him to become prideful, and as a talented cherub he wanted to sit on God's throne. He was prideful because he was not deity and wanted to be (see Isa. 14:12-14). He was arrogant because he was given talents and gifts and wanted them to be more valuable than they actually were. That is why we must have a witness in Heaven and in earth. If you believe that God has called you to a specific duty or talent or gift, two or more must bear witness with you. Yet, if there is no humility, there will not be recognition of this anointing or call on your life. I have seen a lot of people with talents and gifts who never get raised up because of a lack of humility, but I have never seen a person of humility serving someone else who did not get raised up. A few years ago I heard Brian Houston, the pastor of Hillsong Church in Australia, tell a story about how years before they were in need of a worship leader. They found their worship leader in *Darlene Zschech,* who was serving as a secretary on staff. He joked that years later Hillsong music was being sold around the world and *Darlene Zschech* and Hillsong worship was becoming world renown and he, their pastor, was still relatively unknown. Darlene was the right person in the right place at the right time because she had the right heart. I am sure that she had to develop a skill set in order to become one of the world's worship leaders. A humble person will have to develop their skills, talents, and gifts, but it is easier to develop those things than it is to develop an attitude of humility. Every great person has gone through a time of humility, whether it was the wilderness test or the usury test or the lack test or the serving a Saul test. All great leaders or disciples must have their attitude tested and humility established before they can be exalted. God opposes the proud and graces the humble (see James 4:6). The world system doesn't recognize these same principles, so don't buy into the lies of the world. The Kingdom of God's system works, and God will open doors which no man can open after you have been tested and found ready. Starve arrogance and feed humility.

✤ Starve indifference and feed concern. Indifference is passionless and complacent. An indifferent person doesn't live with any urgency whatsoever. Without concern or urgency, there is no drive for achievement, no drive to meet a need. We must be driven to build an organization or build the Kingdom of God. In the beginning, God created man and woman and gave them the command to be fruitful, multiply, subdue, and have dominion as they managed the Garden. Adam and Eve should have concerned themselves with fulfilling the instructions of the Lord. Sometimes innocence can allow for indifference, simply because youthfulness is not as engaged with what is important as an adult would be, opening the innocent up to miss the mark. God needed them to have heart, passion, and urgency toward His commands. If they had possessed the same concern for the Garden and the Kingdom, then they would have been busy keeping the Garden and expanding the Kingdom instead of eating the forbidden fruit. My son at eight years old is not as concerned with keeping his room clean as I am. Why? Possibly because he doesn't have the mental capacity to understand all of the reasons for keeping a clean room. If he discovered organizational discipline, it would create a carefree attitude, allowing my son to be able to find the toys that he wants in a fresh, clean room, which would bring peace to his mother and me! Yet, this is the time of training; we must train him to be concerned with the state of his room. If, after being trained and encouraged, he still doesn't have any concern for these things, he will have developed a careless or indifferent attitude. An indifferent attitude is possible to change, but in order to change indifference, pain must be introduced. By pain I mean the emotion of pain, such as frustration, disappointment, or a motivating factor that says to the person needing to change, "I am not getting anywhere this way" or "I don't like the way that this feels" or "I have got to get a life." Whatever that motivating factor, there must be a "facing of the facts" moment that takes place in an indifferent person's heart and mind. Repentance, turning around, or yielding, will not take place without this recognition. If, as a doctor, I tell you that I have medicine for you and the prescription is ready, there is no concern in your heart or urgency in your soul unless you actually know the diagnosis and the consciousness of what will happen if you do nothing about your condition. Once you know your diagnosis, I can relate to you the prescription for health, because concern and urgency have entered your mind. Repentance will enter into the heart of the unconcerned when they have experienced enough pain. So the worst thing you can do is to rescue an indifferent person from what they don't see or don't care to see. Find their current place of concern and feed that focal point until their whole heart is aware of the consequences of not changing. It may take the pain of losing a job or being rejected on *American Idol* or of someone else being promoted to finally get their attention. No matter what the issue of pain is, ultimately, pain brings awareness of a need, and concern will demand change.

❖ The lack of passion is a product of the lack of dreaming. If you lack passion, you need to feed your curiosity. When I lack passion, I feed my curiosity through meditating on questions like "What would it look like if I...?" One of the passions that I am growing in is my desire to fly an airplane. I ask myself,

"What would it feel like to take off and to land behind the wheel of an airplane?" or "What would it be like to fly my wife to San Francisco for a date?" In order to stimulate your passion, you must stimulate your imagination. Biblical meditation is the art of seeing the invisible as if it were present. Stimulate your curiosity through meditating on, imagining, and dreaming of things that you would love to experience. Find things that cause you to wonder, "What would it feel like to…?"

❧ Starve dishonesty and feed honesty and integrity. Dishonesty and deception (marginal deception or full-fledged lying) are absolutely destructive, disrespectful, and demonic for any team and should be dealt with as if they are cancer: completely cut out. Marginal deception is particularly destructive because the truth is only partially disclosed; it's the truth with omission. Dishonesty comes from a crooked or shameful heart. Both of these motivations need to be dealt with. Honesty and integrity are difficult standards to live by, yet they are not optional. The choice to live by deception is the same choice that satan made in betraying God, or that Judas made in betraying Jesus, or that Peter made in denying that he knew Jesus. When you can easily blow off a small lie or omit some of the truth, then you have made a journey to the dark side. If you don't quickly make a change, you will find out how easy it is to keep going down that dead-end road—all the while thinking that you have gotten away with something. Your leader needs complete honesty; if you didn't get the work done, be honest.

Don't make up "the dog ate my work stories," or "I thought that you meant," or "I told so-and-so to get it done; they didn't do it?" These things will cause a change in your position on the team as soon as your leader sees the opportunity to replace you with an honest person. Feed honesty, and you gain the respect of the leader and of the team. Feed integrity, and you will feel better about yourself and your future. Honesty and integrity will always look to speak the truth; sometimes it will be tough, but if you can overcome and press through to victory, then God will see your faithfulness and reward you. Pretenders and con artists will be found out and eventually judged. Take the high road. We are children of the King, and His Holy Spirit lives within us; we don't need to live in deception and half-truths. Let's rise above the world's system of deception and step into the Kingdom's demand of living above reproach. Let's starve perversion, which is the distortion of truth, and feed sincerity, which is the pursuit of being like Christ.

❧ Starve rebellion and feed submission. Lucifer's fall from Heaven gives us a striking picture of the reward of rebellion. God refused to tolerate rebellion on His team. Rebellion was not only confronted, but rebellion was expelled. We must have the same heart. We cannot tolerate rebellion, no matter how talented or gifted an individual is; a wrong attitude must immediately be kicked out. Your leader needs you to be submissive. I had to make some tough decisions in the early part of my ministry. I was submitted to my pastor as a youth pastor at the Life Church under Pastors Phil and Jeannie Munsey, but I felt the call to travel and to move on in ministry. My pastor did not feel that it was time, but I insisted that it was time, so I resigned my position and left the work. Three weeks later, the Lord challenged me to go and submit to another pastor in a nearby city; I refused because I was going to be a big traveling minister to the nations. Rebellion was beginning to grow in my heart. Within the following three weeks, all of my three speaking engagements were canceled, and I needed to make a choice. I called the ministry in the nearby city. In arrogance, I told him that I could only serve for six months because I was going to be traveling full time. Two years later he released me to travel full time. One year later, I woke up to God's voice saying, "Go to the Life Church this morning." I was not happy about that! But I had learned a little bit, so I said, "God, speak to my wife about it." A few minutes later, my wife woke up and said, "I think that we should go to the Life Church this morning." So we did. As we walked in, Pastor Phil welcomed us like we were lost children finding our way home. This was in 1997; we have been submitted and serving Pastors Phil and Jeannie ever since, and God has blessed us richly because of the submission. I have had to make the tough journey of humility with many pastors because I was so arrogant and rebellious. I have been both rebellious and submitted; I have found so much more grace under submission than I ever have under rebellion. God made me go back and make things right, because when I left, my heart was not right. Rebellion didn't start in my heart as a Christian. Rebellion was in my heart as a son, as a student, as a player on the football field. I didn't have success in those areas because I didn't know how to submit, and when I came into the Kingdom, that same mind-set of rebellion stuck with me, until I was challenged to submit. I had to renew my mind to submission in order to break through the rebellion. I described it as independence or creativity or my "call," but it was all rebellion. The only way to break the cycle of rebellion is through submission. Really submit once, and you will destroy the heart of rebellion for good. I am not saying that you won't be challenged to rebel, but if you have learned submission, you will understand authority. True authority comes from submission, true favor comes through submission, and true freedom is only known in submission. Remember the centurion: *"For I also am a man under authority, having soldiers under me. And I say to this one, 'Go,' and he goes; and to another, 'Come,' and he comes"* (Matt. 8:9). If you want authority, learn to live under authority. Learn to live as a servant, and you will learn what it means to have authority. The moment I really submitted, I broke a destructive pattern in my life, and you can do the same if this is your issue. Your submission cannot be different from one day to another; there is no such thing as fickle submission. Submission is a choice. As a submitted person, you make a commitment to your leader, to the team, and to the work at hand.

❖ Starve impatience and feed patience. The Bible says in the Book of James, *"But let patience have its perfect work, that you may be perfect and complete, lacking nothing"* (James 1:4). Patience has a work to do in all of us, and her job description is to mature us, complete us, and destroy lack in every area of our lives. Impatience prolongs immaturity, keeps you from peace, and keeps you defiant in every area of your life. Patience can only benefit those who will allow her to work. I often hear people talk about how impatient they can be, even pompously as if it is a fruit of the Spirit. Patience, not impatience, is a fruit of the Spirit. Patience doesn't work alone, as we see in Romans 5:3-5: *"And not only so, but we glory in tribulations also: knowing that tribulation worketh patience; and patience, experience; and experience, hope: and hope maketh not ashamed; because the love of God is shed abroad in our hearts by the Holy Ghost which is given unto us"* (KJV). Patience is set up by tribulation; tribulation works on you and prepares you for the arrival of patience. Then, once patience starts working on you, experience will join the fun. We all must understand that experience is a vital part of our lives: until we experience limitation, we will not fully comprehend our potential; until we experience failure, we will not understand how needed success is in our lives; and until we experience submission, we will never be a strong leader. Experience is key; without it, you will never be introduced to hope. Hope acts as a barrier to keep shame from your life. Hope keeps you focused on what is possible. If you experience something that is designed to create hope within you, and you don't receive that experience as a time of training, it will do just the opposite. Instead of building hope, it will make your heart grow sick. If you see the experience as training, then you will understand that training comes to prepare you for something greater than the season that you are currently living in. Impatience is the by-product of a person's hope being deferred.

Keep hope alive and live according to a higher mandate, a greater law of victory. Hope will keep us from giving in to improper desires, which fight against our souls.

> *Dear friends, I warn you as "temporary residents and foreigners" to keep away from worldly desires that wage war against your very souls* (1 Peter 2:11 NLT).

Evil is like cancer; it's aggressive and destructive. Jesus said to Peter that the devil wanted to sift him like wheat (see Luke 22:31-32). The enemy wants to sift you and me like wheat. The enemy's process of sifting starts in the mind. My own battle with anxiety started with just one thought that I didn't get under control. After some time, that one thought of fear took more and more of my thought life until I was consumed with fear. Seek first the Kingdom of God and its righteousness, and God will add to you everything needed (see Matt. 6:33).

CHAPTER NINE

PROSPEROUS THINKING

YOUR ATTITUDE CONTROLS THE way you think. Negative attitudes will give way to fear and unbelief. A prosperous attitude will give way to confidence and positive thinking. The Bible says it this way: *"be renewed in the spirit of your mind, and...put on the new man which was created according to God, in true righteousness and holiness"* (Eph. 4:23-24).

We all can be renewed in the spirit of our mind, in the attitudes of our mind, and in the way that we think. Prosperous thinking is not the same as positive thinking. Positive thinking tries to keep a bright side perspective on all things; we should all have that way of thinking. A prosperous thinker thinks of ways that will move things forward even during challenging times and does not just accept that something wrong has happened. The prosperous thinker never says, "Oh well, let's look on the bright side of things." It is what Napoleon Hill, in his book *Think and Grow Rich,* called looking for an equivalent benefit in a negative or challenging circumstance. A prosperous mind looks for opportunities rather than deficiencies in challenging times. Prosperity means to advance. Prosperous thinkers are always looking for an opportunity to advance themselves, their leaders, and the Kingdom of God. Without this mind-set, disciples can become stagnant and unproductive. They will get bogged down in the messes of life, become unfit for the Kingdom of God, and useless to their leaders. The Kingdom of God must always grow, especially since the Kingdom of God is within us. Without an advancing mind-set, the Kingdom of God will be held hostage by an unproductive life. Serve with an advancing mind-set. Love your spouse with an advancing mind-set. Raise your children with an advancing mind-set. This mind-set doesn't ask, "Why did this happen to me?" in a complaining way. This mind-set goes on a fact-finding mission by asking, "What should I be learning from this so that I can advance myself, my family, my leader, and the Kingdom of God?" Positive thinking alone will not achieve anything. Without action to bring about the equivalent benefit, you are just going to be positive. Looking for the equivalent benefit serves as a call to action. Sitting still and looking positively at your circumstance is a positive-thinking strategy, but moving toward a beneficial outcome is a prosperous mind-set.

Prosperous thinking is a combination of a positive attitude, strategic forward thinking, and thinking outside of the box. In addition to prosperous thinking, prosperous thinkers take big action in order to achieve their desired results. Results are only produced by action; to change the result you must change the action. Poverty action produces disastrous results, good intentions produce mediocre results, excellent action produces good results, and outstanding action produces excellent results. When I was in high school I played football. I was a halfback, wide receiver, and safety. I could run a 4.5 40 and I had lots of jukes and moves. One day in a game I received a hand off that resulted in a zero yardage gain. My coach later said, "You have a lot of moves and skills but you lack initiative." The truth is that I didn't practice with initiative, I did not workout with initiative, and neither did I show initiative in the game. I grew up in a house of athletes, two-time Olympians, golden glove champions, and football rushing record holders who attended that same high school years earlier. I remember when I joined the football team; the coaches were very excited that I was an

Armstrong. Physically I had the same talent, but mentally I didn't have the same determination. I put in good effort and received poor results. My family members put in outstanding efforts with the same skills and achieved excellence. This was a huge lesson for me. I have learned that Olympians live by a different action level than a common athlete. Amongst Olympic athletes you will find a level playing field regarding skill sets, but the thing that separates one from another just may be the difference in internal intensity.

You will always have to put more into your action than you expect back. This is a prosperous mind-set and will be hard to swallow for mediocre thinkers. If you are comfortable now, you will have to put in more action to stay where you are. People think that if they don't do anything differently they will maintain, yet maintenance demands that you do one step above where you are currently to stay there. Otherwise, you will fall back one step by doing nothing. It is called atrophy. Atrophy is when the muscles that you once used to achieve the level of your current stature are no longer being used; they begin to stiffen and weaken, becoming useless and powerless. The deterioration begins after passivity, and you lose the muscle that you had once gained. This happens in your body but also in the spirit, soul, and mind.

A few years ago I read a newspaper article that explored the world of Alzheimer's patients. This article claimed that constantly challenging your brain to learn and think of new things would combat Alzheimer's disease. Think prosperously and keep your mind. Prosperous thinking will not allow you to be negative or bitter. There is no advancement or benefit to mankind or to the Kingdom of God through negativity or bitterness; wage war on it today and live a prosperous life.

The Word of God says, *"Beloved, I pray that you may prosper in all things and be in health, just as your soul prospers"* (3 John 2).

This means that God desires for us to prosper, but first in our souls.

God has designed it so that you are a product of your soul. If you are not prosperous or advancing, it is because your soul is not advancing. To advance is a conscious decision. You may win the lottery and get rich, but until you have the soul that can handle riches you will not be prosperous. Make sure that you are emotionally and mentally prospering so that you will prosper in every area of your life. Make sure that you laugh loudly and think deeply every day to keep your soul prosperous. Take off your shoes and walk barefoot in the grass on a regular basis to release stress in your soul and body.

I know that we covered this earlier, but I must say it again: seek the Lord daily with all of your heart to have a prosperous soul. This is the will of God. God will give quick and early success to those who seek Him; the precedent has been set in Second Chronicles 26:3-5:

> *Uzziah was sixteen years old when he began his fifty-two-year reign in Jerusalem. His mother was Jecoliah of Jerusalem. He did right in the Lord's sight, to the extent of all that his father Amaziah had done. He set himself to seek God in the days of Zechariah, who instructed him in the things of God; and as long as he sought (inquired of, yearned for) the Lord, God made him prosper* (AMP).

Prosperity is a by-product of wisdom. God has wisdom for you as you advance in life, in leadership, and in the Kingdom of God.

CHAPTER TEN

ARCHITECTS AND BUILDERS

I planted, Apollos watered, but God gave the increase. So then neither
he who plants is anything, nor he who waters, but God who gives the
increase. Now he who plants and he who waters are one, and each one
will receive his own reward according to his own labor. For we are God's
fellow workers; you are God's field, you are God's building. According to
the grace of God which was given to me, as a wise master builder I have
laid the foundation, and another builds on it. But let each one take heed
how he builds on it (1 Corinthians 3:6-10).

Alignment

I WANT TO SPEND some time breaking down these verses, starting with
the first two. The apostle's words have to do with *alignment*:

> *I planted, Apollos watered, but God gave the increase. So*
> *then neither he who plants is anything, nor he who waters,*

but God who gives the increase. Now he who plants and he who waters are one, and each one will receive his own reward according to his own labor (1 Corinthians 3:6-8).

One thing that we must learn to do in the Kingdom of God is to align ourselves with one another, utilizing our strength to become a force to be reckoned with in the earth. If you look around, you will see alignment taking place in the corporate world on a daily basis. Taco Bell and Pizza Hut, grocery stores and banks, KFC and A&W, all use each other's customer base to capture more market share and increase profits. They have found strength in serving each other as they each service their customers. In order to be a great servant, you must first believe that you possess something great to give. Read Matthew 20:23-28 with this perspective:

Jesus said to them, "You will indeed drink from My cup, but to sit at My right or left is not for Me to grant. These places belong to those for whom they have been prepared by My Father." When the ten heard about this, they were indignant with the two brothers. Jesus called them together and said, "You know that the rulers of the Gentiles lord it over them, and their high officials exercise authority over them. Not so with you. Instead, whoever wants to become great among you must be your servant, and whoever wants to be first must be your slave—just as the Son of Man did not come to be served, but to serve, and to give His life as a ransom for many" (NIV).

The subject is greatness, not smallness. If you're great, then you must have something to offer; the objective then becomes serving out of the greatness that you possess. Only big people can serve; only great people can serve. People who feel the call of greatness have a mandate to first discover the soul of serving. David found that he had something to give and used his greatness to serve his generation and fulfill the will of God:

> *For David, after he had served his own generation by the*
> *will of God, fell asleep, was buried with his fathers, and saw*
> *corruption* (Acts 13:36).

Aligning your greatness with someone else's greatness will create a synergy that brings increase:

> *Behold, how good and how pleasant it is for brethren to dwell*
> *together in unity! It is like the precious oil upon the head,*
> *running down on the beard, the beard of Aaron, running*
> *down on the edge of his garments. It is like the dew of Hermon,*
> *descending upon the mountains of Zion; for there the Lord*
> *commanded the blessing—life forevermore* (Psalm 133:1-3).

The blessing of increase is consistently found in alignment. No one gets the sole credit for the increase, yet each will be rewarded for the progress.

Farmers and Builders

Moving on to First Corinthians 3:9, we have a chance to understand God's thoughts on farming and building: *"For we are God's fellow workers; you are God's field, you are God's building."* God is a farmer and a builder. A farmer understands what it is to go through the cultivation process with an ethic of hard work. The planting and sowing process precedes the enjoyment of the increase of a harvest. As farmers, we must understand the process of sowing and reaping. Being a farmer is very different from being a mechanic. A mechanic finds a problem and fixes it to see instant results. A farmer tills the ground, sows the seeds, waters the ground, removes the weeds, and harvests the increase. God is systematic, and we must also become systematic, whether it comes naturally or is developed as a skill.

Additionally, we must become builders, just as God is a builder. We must not only think like farmers, but we must also think like builders. A builder is strategic, working from an architect's drawings that show what the building should look like. A builder also prepares the ground, sets the foundation, sets the framework, adds a roof, and completes it with detailed finishes. A builder doesn't veer away from the architectural drawings; if he does, he will endanger the entire project. The farmer works with the natural flow of organic and living materials, learning how to flow with the universal laws to get things done. The builder works with non-organic materials and produces things on purpose that have long-lasting value.

Wise Master Builders

The last point is from verse 10, which says, *"According to the grace of God which was given to me, as a wise master builder I have laid the foundation, and another builds on it. But let each one take heed how he builds on it."* When we become builders, God gives us grace to build as wise master builders. *Master builder* comes from the Greek word *architekton* (ar-khee-tek'-tone) which means "a chief constructor," "architect."[1] As wise master builders, we must learn to do things purposefully, strategically, and creatively. Build with the wisdom of the Ancient of days; build with the idea that whatever you are building will last forever. The more spiritual you are, the more purposeful and strategic you must become. A lack of purpose caused Adam and Eve to deviate from the original plan and turn humankind upside down. So it will take wise and purposeful building to return things to normal. Christ's coming and death was not an accident; it was a product of architectural design. Your leader and your future leadership will benefit from your wisdom. Chief constructors always build with a mind-set that what they are building will last. Architects are creative; they want to see what they have imagined come to life. Think creatively and establish systems and processes that will produce your harvest.

Endnote

1. "Architekton"; http://www.studylight.org/lex/grk/view.cgi?number=753.

PART 3

LIFESTYLE

CHAPTER ELEVEN

BALANCED LIVING

Does He not see my ways and count my every step? If I have walked in falsehood or my foot has hurried after deceit—let God weigh me in honest scales and He will know that I am blameless (Job 31:4-6 NIV).

Right Balances

CONGRUENCY IS A WORD that we need to use more frequently in the Kingdom of God. We all would have a hard time if God were not congruent. For example, when I was young I was a Muslim. One of the things that I found disheartening as a Muslim was that I would pray five times a day toward the east, starting at 5:00 A.M. and ending at bedtime, and never once received an answer or heard even the smallest instruction. This to me was incongruent. In order for people to believe in you and for you to be attractive so that people will want to align themselves with you, there must not be any area that is not growing and developing. If you are growing spiritually and you're not advancing in your soul emotionally or mentally, then you are not living a congruent lifestyle. If you have a healthy soul and great spiritual development, yet you eat as if you have no self-control or consideration for the temple of the Holy Spirit, then you will not have a congruent lifestyle. We must express control in every area of our lives. I am not saying that we will be perfect in every area, but we must be in pursuit of balanced living. We must try to bring balance to our spirit, soul, and bodies so that we will be as effective as we can be. Unbalanced areas are highly susceptible to pitfalls that can bring devastation to you and your organization.

Strive for excellence in every area: spiritually, physically, emotionally, mentally; in your family, ministry, and recreation. Keeping a balanced life is the best thing that you can do for yourself and your leader. We cannot rationalize and make excuses for the conflicts of our souls and our actions. Our mind-set must match our actions; for example, a doctor who smokes, yet warns his patients about smoking, has a double standard that waters down his effectiveness and credibility. God abhors imbalance; we see this in the Book of Proverbs *"A false balance and unrighteous dealings are extremely offensive and shamefully sinful to the Lord, but a just weight is His delight"* (Prov. 11:1 AMP).

Healthy Boundaries

In the same way that we should keep right balances, we should also keep healthy boundaries. What is a healthy boundary? Boundaries are associated with our comfort zones. Each one of us lives with some degree of a comfort zone; some people have larger comfort zones than others. Our comfort zone regulates how we relate to others, our environment, and opportunities. The way we see ourselves affects our performance on the job, in sports, or in anything else that we do. Sometimes a person with a low self-image will allow people with an exaggerated self-image to violate his comfort zone and overstep his boundaries. He tolerates things that anyone with a strong self-understanding would never tolerate. This tolerance may be associated with his upbringing or an unhealthy relationship from the past. If you tolerate uncomfortable people and circumstances without confronting the issue, eventually you will encounter control or manipulation. You may also lose control of your self-confidence and defer your decisions and opinions to whomever will take control. Eventually you will become numb to the pain and give your life to someone else to live. Our boundaries move and flex. Each day we are defending, expanding, fortifying, or collapsing boundaries to make another comfort zone or to maintain one.

Broken Boundaries

When someone breaks a boundary, you feel it immediately; at that very instant you are forced to make some choices: allow that person to stay and rewrite the boundary lines, reject and kick him out, or freeze up and become ineffective. You will feel the same thing when asked to perform something that you have never done in the ministry or on the job. What happens to a person who has never spoken in front of a crowd and is asked to give a speech next week in front of the board? That's right—she is moved out of her comfort zone, and physiology confirms it. She begins to sweat, even though it is a week away; she gets short of breath, and pictures of choking up and failing miserably flash into her mind. She sees herself walking out of the office with all of her belongings in a box. As soon as you are moved out of your comfort zone, your performance lowers because of a lack of confidence, and you begin to look for a way out, thinking, "Maybe I can call in sick that day."

Moving Your Boundary Lines

Most people don't know why they feel the way they do when a boundary line has been broken. Most people subconsciously have boundaries usually associated with their upbringing, their environment, or their self-image. We must learn to recognize when these boundaries are being pushed, either in a good way or in a bad way. Once, I approached one of our ministry students, saying, "I want you to lead worship tonight." She graciously declined the opportunity because she was not a worship leader nor did she feel comfortable singing. I didn't mind that she didn't want to lead worship that night; I was just joking with her because our worship leader was running late. A few days later she came to me and said, "Pastor, I am sorry that I declined to sing. I went home and felt like the Holy Spirit challenged me to never turn down an opportunity to serve you when it arises, no matter how nervous I am, because it will stretch me and make me better." Since then, this woman has always taken on the challenges set before her and has risen within our ranks as a leader. Even at her job she has out-performed her coworkers and has moved up the ladder to a management position because she will not run from a challenge due to boundaries set by her insecurity or fear. She purposely moves her boundary lines and rises to the challenge to achieve great things. You might feel uncomfortable at first, but eventually your comfort zone will rise to a higher level.

We have control of our spirit. One day I was speaking to a person who said that she couldn't stop a destructive behavior, so I asked her why. She said because it was hard. I asked her, "How did you start it?" She told me how, and I said, "Now you know how to stop it. You chose to start it; now choose to stop it." Why couldn't she stop? She had moved her boundary lines and created a new comfort zone for herself. I said, "So make that decision!" She responded, "But my boyfriend and my friends wouldn't understand." She decided to take control, and began attending a support group that fortified her newfound comfort zone.

Often our associations will have to be changed in order to move our boundaries where they should be to establish that new comfort zone. Take charge of your life and regain control of your destiny by establishing new boundaries and walls in your life. As Proverbs 25:28 says, *"He who has no rule over his own spirit is like a city that is broken down and without walls"* (AMP). These walls are not just to keep the wrong things out, but to help keep the right things in. Don't lose your throne; continue to rule your emotions, imagination, and comfort zones so that you can achieve what God has designed for you. Remember, dream of and take challenges that will cause you to progress. Raise the wall of resistance that will keep out people who have wrong agendas that can hurt you. When your body and nervous system begin to talk to you, ask, "Why do I feel this way?" Then hunt it down. Never ignore these responses; something has triggered these warning signals. You must investigate and judge it according to the Word of God and the fruit of the Holy Spirit.

Health and Balance

Make healthy eating and physical exercise a daily part of your balanced living. You may be thinking "How can this help me serve my leader?" First of all, your leader doesn't need someone who is always tired and sluggish, complaining that everything is too much. Leaders need people who are alive and ready to go. Secondly, they also need you to be confident if you are overweight. I recently read an article online, "Health Effects of Being Overweight: The Dangerous Truth" by Rajeevk. I have included a quote from the article:

> Weight and health are strongly related to each other. The risk of disease goes up as weight gain pushes you out of the healthy weight range and into the overweight, obese range. Till date, obesity has been linked with more than thirty medical conditions. Not just large weight gains carry ill health effects; even 10 or 20 extra pounds increase the risk of disease and death. The health effects of being overweight are dangerous and hazardous to life.[1]

In addition to adverse health problems, which seem to be more than we understand, being overweight can also affect a person's self-image. It may change the way you feel in your favorite dress or the way you feel because you can no longer button the button on your dress shirt, which could in turn affect your self-confidence. A low self-confidence can also affect your performance. Being overweight doesn't represent godly discipline and diligence. We must look as if we have consciously picked out what we wear and what we put in our bodies; we must represent the best that the Kingdom of God has to offer. We must also get the right amount of sleep. I have worked with people all over the world and have found that oversleeping can make a person feel sluggish, while under-sleeping can make a person nervous. We must eat the right foods: energy and nutrient dense foods for the body. Add more green and colored raw foods to your diet; it will give you more energy than fatty and fried foods or simple carbohydrates. If you really want to be at the top of your game, you should stop eating pork. The effects of eating pork are widely published. I have included a few things that I had never heard before in the following quote:

> Swine are also good incubators of toxic parasites and viruses—although the animal doesn't appear to be ill while carrying these diseases. A scientist at the University of Giessen's Institute for Virology in Germany showed in a study of worldwide influenza epidemics that pigs are the one animal that can serve as a mixing vessel for new influenza viruses that may seriously threaten world health. If a pig is exposed to a human's DNA virus and then a bird's virus, the pig mixes the two viruses—developing a new DNA virus that is often extremely lethal for humans. These viruses have already caused worldwide epidemics and destruction. Virologists have concluded that if we do not find a way to separate humans from pigs, the whole earth's population may be at risk.[2]

In his book *The Maker's Diet*, Dr. Jordan Rubin quotes Elmer Josephson, author of *God's Key to Health and Happiness*:

> Some ask, why did the Lord make the unclean animals? They were created as scavengers. As a rule they are meat-eating animals that clean up anything that is left dead in the fields, etc., but scavengers were never created for human consumption. The flesh of the swine is said by many authorities to be the prime cause of much of our American ill health, causing blood diseases, weakness of the stomach, liver troubles, eczema, consumption, tumors, cancer, etc.
>
> The scale less fish and all shell fish including the oyster, clam, lobster, shrimp, etc., modern science discovers to be lumps of devitalized and disease producing filth, because of inadequate excretion. These are the scavengers, and the garbage containers of the waters and the sea.[3]

Research the effects of pork on the body for yourself. Research how they get rid of their waste and realize that they don't have a way to sweat out the toxins, which is the very reason that the meat is so salty. Research how it is prepared and how many tumors are allowed to be in the meat at the butcher. It will shock you! There is a reason for why the Bible calls this animal unclean. *The Hog: Should It Be Used for Food?*, a book written by C. Leonard Vories, is an excellent read that will cause you to re-think your annual holiday meat or daily lunchmeat. Let's work hard to go back to the Bible in every area of our lives, including the temple of the Holy Spirit: our body. Our Savior didn't eat swine; why should we? Why should we die early and miss our calls as many mighty men and women of God have done because of a dysfunctional, uneducated relationship with food and an inability to control our comfort zone? Let us live by design and not by default.

If you smoke, work hard to stop, not only because it is a sin against your body, but also because it is not successful. Success is all about increase, and smoking only decreases. Smoking decreases your lung capacity, your heart health, and your life expectancy. When I was young, a doctor brought photos to our church of a lung of a smoker and a lung of a non-smoker. The smoker's lungs were stained black by the nicotine tar and had a shriveled appearance, and the non-smoker's lungs were clean and pink and strong-looking. I remember thinking, "I don't ever want to have black lungs!" I found some shocking statistics from the Center for Disease Control and Prevention. Their research has revealed the following:

> The adverse health effects from cigarette smoking account for an estimated 443,000 deaths, or nearly 1 of every 5 deaths, each year in the United States. More deaths are caused each year by tobacco use than by all deaths from human immunodeficiency virus (HIV), illegal drug use, alcohol use, motor vehicle injuries, suicides, and murders combined.

> Smoking Causes Death

> Smoking causes approximately:

> 90% of all *lung cancer* deaths in men

> 80% of all *lung cancer* deaths in women

> 90% of deaths from *chronic obstructive lung disease*

> Smoking causes the following cancers:

> *acute myeloid leukemia*

> *kidney cancer*

cancer of the pancreas

bladder cancer

cancer of the larynx (voice box)

cancer of the pharynx (throat)

cancer of the cervix

lung cancer

stomach cancer

cancer of the esophagus

cancer of the oral cavity (mouth)

cancer of the uterus

Smoking harms nearly every organ of the body. Smoking causes many diseases and reduces the health of smokers in general.[4]

The same goes for alcohol. Don't stop drinking simply because it is a sin; stop because you have a great work to accomplish, and you want to fulfill it with peak performance and health.

Learn to dress for success. If you don't know how to dress for success, then ask your leaders how they would like for you to dress. If your leader doesn't have a revelation of the need for a successful appearance, then go to a book store and buy a fashion magazine that won't make you blush or sin by reading it, and learn how to be an attractive helper and leader. Make sure that you take showers daily, and for heaven's sake, brush your teeth more than once a day. Also, carry a pack of gum or breath mints at all times. Never allow your leader to be without breath mints. When talking closely, slip a mint into your mouth to be polite. Please wash, cut, style, and condition your hair. Hygiene, hygiene, hygiene: at all times think hygiene. Be as fashion forward as your budget will allow. You may have to watch The Learning Channel to get some fashion advice on how to stay fashion forward on a budget. It helps the people you are leading and serving not to be repelled by your odor or appearance, and will keep you focused on your task without concern for these things.

I know that many will think that this is a shallow part of this book, but it still needs to be said. We have preachers and other ministers going to an early grave because they cannot say no to fried chicken and pork chops, and the devil has nothing to do with it. It comes back to our comfort zones and the authority that we have in the kingdom of our souls.

These things are soul issues. Change your soul regarding them and live a healthy and prosperous life.

> *Beloved, I pray that you may prosper in all things and be in health, just as your soul prospers* (3 John 2).

Endnotes

1. Rajeevk, "Health Effects of Being Overweight: The Dangerous Truth"; http://www.articlealley.com/article_809557_23.html.

2. Paul Wong, "Eating Pork can be Hazardous to your Health"; http://www.onlinetruth.org/Articles%20Folder/eating_pork_can_be_hazardous_to.htm.

3. Quoted in Dr. Jordan Rubin, *The Maker's Diet* (Berkley Trade, 2005).

4. See Centers for Disease Control and Prevention, "Health Effects of Cigarette Smoking" ; http://www.cdc.gov/tobacco/data_statistics/fact_sheets/health_effects/effects_cig_smoking/index.htm.

CHAPTER TWELVE

WIN FRIENDS, INFLUENCE PEOPLE, AND CHERISH YOUR FAMILY

ONE OF THE GREATEST things that you can learn as support to a leader is to win friends and attract people. The Bible says that if you're a friendly person, you will have friends (see Prov. 18:24). Being friendly, attracting friends, and maintaining friends is a big thing in the ministry. Whether they are friends of the ministry or personal friends, without friendliness you will not have any friends. You must learn to be outgoing; even as an introvert, you must learn to communicate with a smile and friendly tones. These are skills and choices. Choose to be friendly. While traveling, I have run into door Nazis, platform-step Nazis, pastor Nazis, and guest-speaker Nazis. Sometimes I think that these people get so caught up in their duties that they have forgotten why they even help in the ministry: ministry means serving.

As a minister of helping, one of your greatest assets is to be friendly. No matter how important your job is or how strict your policy is, you can choose how sternly you enforce it. I did away with the security team at our church because, walking around like a militia, they were scary and intimidating to

FOLLOWERSHIP

our visitors. They don't have to look mean. We must welcome the friends and guests of our ministries and treat them accordingly. When I go to Disneyland, they have security people everywhere, probably the best in the world, and I have never felt afraid of them. I respect them and want them around, but I have no problem asking them for directions, either. Remember that as servant to the minister you are a representative to the friends and guests of the ministry or organization. If you are unfriendly and intimidating, I can guarantee that the organization will suffer in the long run, if it hasn't already.

Make sure that you personally know how to win friends, that you have friends that you can fellowship with, and that you know some unbelievers that you can be friendly with. In the public eye and in the house of God, you should always come across as friendly. Our goal is to win people, not just be friends with Christians. In my life I have purposefully joined fitness clubs in order to keep relationships outside of the church where I pastor. I also go to coffee with my neighbor, who is not a Christian at this point in his life, so that I can have a chance to get to know him and hopefully be an example of Christ's love. In our church we have adopted a "circle of three" concept called "The One." The One campaign encourages each believer to pray for and pastor three people whom we consider un-churched or far from God; one friend, one family member, and one neighbor. The goal is to be compassionate and focus on meaningful listening as we engage these relationships, awaiting the opportunity to share the love of Christ. We have made this campaign free for any pastor who would like to introduce it to his church. If all of your friends are Christians and you don't go out of your way to meet new people, then you are not winning souls. I am absolutely not suggesting that you live a sinful life with them. I am suggesting that you don't become isolated to the point that you are unable to befriend an unsaved person in order to win them to Christ. As Paul the apostle said,

> *Though I am free and belong to no man, I make myself a*
> *slave to everyone, to win as many as possible. To the Jews I*

130

became like a Jew, to win the Jews. To those under the law
I became like one under the law (though I myself am not
under the law), so as to win those under the law. To those
not having the law I became like one not having the law
(though I am not free from God's law but am under Christ's
law), so as to win those not having the law. To the weak I
became weak, to win the weak. I have become all things to
all men so that by all possible means I might save some. I
do all this for the sake of the gospel, that I may share in its
blessings (1 Corinthians 9:19-23 NIV).

The Power of Friendliness

Being friendly is a strategy. Learn to influence people through your friendliness. When you meet someone new for the first time, make sure that you use their name in a sentence three or four times during your conversation. Also, make sure that you don't dominate the conversation talking about yourself and your life; be sincerely interested in them and listen intently. Fight the urge to put in your two cents worth and don't constantly lean the conversation back toward your life. Be especially careful not to interrupt them in the middle of a sentence; doing so would be rude and unfriendly. After they have answered a question about themselves, ask another one. People love to talk about themselves and hear their name spoken in conversation. If you have a hard time remembering names, write their name down on a piece of paper when you walk away so that you can pray for them later or surprise them by remembering their name later. These are just a few ideas, but I encourage you to pick up the book *How to Win Friends and Influence People* by Dale Carnegie to learn more skills.[1] Being friendly is a strategy; you have to choose to be friendly on purpose. The key is to be consistent in your friendliness. If you are friendly three weeks in a row and the fourth week you let a negative emotion take control, that one slip will be what people remember much longer than any of your previous friendly acts.

Friendliness will introduce you to people who will eventually become more than just associates. They will be your covenant partners. This truth is found in Proverbs 18:24: *"A man who has friends must himself be friendly, but there is a friend who sticks closer than a brother."* Although "through-thick-and-thin" friends and true covenant partners are hard to find, when you develop that relationship, it will be a blessing to you and your descendants.

Choosing Friends Wisely

The company you keep determines your future; you must learn to carefully choose and keep your friends on purpose. This is a hard principle for many to digest. Let those whom you fellowship and associate with be people who will challenge you to become who you are destined to be in the future. If you are careless about how and with whom you spend time, you will find that the moment you want to break away to do something of significance, you will have a hard time doing so.

There are three main things that I want to instill into my children's belief system. If they get these three things, they will never fail in life, walk away from God, or miss achieving their dreams. First, I want them to always obey God. Second, I want them to know that their attitude is everything; and third, I want them to understand that they must learn to choose and influence the right friends and relationships. If they will major in these three things, their lives will take off, and they will do great things for God. We must choose friends with good habits and strong disciplines; one choice to have the wrong company can destroy all of these things. First Corinthians 15:33 says, *"Do not be deceived: 'Evil company corrupts good habits.'"* Negative people love to keep company with negative people;

in the same manner, positive people keep company with positive people. Judge yourself by taking note of those with whom you keep company. People take note, and will see you in the same light as the people you allow close in your life.

The Art of Influence

You can influence people, or they can influence you. To influence someone, you must understand the boundaries of the relationship. When I am around people whom I admire, who have great character, a positive attitude, and a go-getter lifestyle, I am always open to be influenced by them. Yet, if I am around someone who is just the opposite of me, I realize that I must take the lead and influence them toward their future and toward living their best life. Know when you have to make the switch from servant to leader and leader to servant. This will help you in the long run to be an influencer of people in a good way instead of being corrupted by evil company.

Your ability to influence people will be a necessary and vital asset to your leader and the organization. If you can posture yourself to serve your leader with a mind to also gather and lead others, you will benefit the leader more than simply being a task-oriented helper. Leader-servants are hard enough to find, and any good leader would do whatever is necessary to keep a leader-servant on the team. What is a leader-servant? My understanding of a leader-servant is someone who has made a mental and emotional transition from serving through their own ability, to leading while serving through others. Of course this type of transition is conscious and purposeful and could even be difficult at first, but once this mind-set becomes second nature, your whole life will be more efficient and effective.

Jesus Himself needed to make this shift. We see the process in Matthew 9:27-34. Paul the apostle based his whole ministry on his ability to draw people into emulation, which resulted in them serving the Lord with all of their heart. As we have already read, Paul deliberately made himself attractive to all men so that he may save some. In Romans 11:13-14, he says, *"I am talking to you Gentiles. Inasmuch as I am the apostle to the Gentiles, I make much of my ministry in the hope that I may somehow arouse my own people to envy and save some of them"* (NIV). He uses the word *parazeloo* (par-ad-zay-lo'-o), which means "to provoke to jealousy or rivalry."[2] To influence people is to stimulate them alongside, to get them involved, whether they do it out of jealousy or excitement; the Gospel must be preached and people must be reached. Of course, we absolutely don't want ill-motivated people operating in our ministry because of the law of reproduction that would follow.

As I mentioned already, attitude, along with results, are the primary markers for evaluation. If a person has a bad attitude and bad results, he or she must be removed immediately. We can hopefully move a person who has bad results into a new position in order to help them find a place where they can flourish, but a negative attitude must be cut out like cancer. We must understand that everyone will have different motivations for serving; some will serve because they are gifted with mercy, some will serve with a desire for significance, etc. To think that everyone will have the same motivation is foolish, yet we should rejoice that the work is being done, even as Paul did in Philippians 1:15-18:

> *It is true that some preach Christ out of envy and rivalry, but others out of goodwill. The latter do so in love, knowing that I am put here for the defense of the gospel. The former preach Christ out of selfish ambition, not sincerely, supposing that they can stir up trouble for me while I am in chains. But what does it matter? The important thing is that in every way, whether from false motives or true, Christ is preached. And because of this I rejoice* (NIV).

Study Paul's writings, and you will discover the art of influence. Paul was so influential that he nearly persuaded King Agrippa. The King's response to visiting with Paul as a prisoner was, *"Almost thou persuadest me to be a Christian"* (Acts 26:28 KJV). Develop the art of persuasion; your leader needs to know that you are a go-getter who can get people involved to "getter done." John Maxwell in his book *Developing the Leader Within You* says that leadership is influence.[3] Leader servanthood is then the ability to influence people to join the cause as you serve your leader and the cause. There will come a point in your progression when your serving becomes influential.

Starting at Home

The best place to improve your serving and influence abilities is at home. Paul sets a challenging standard in First Timothy 3:4-5:

> *He must manage his own family well and see that his children obey him with proper respect. (If anyone does not know how to manage his own family, how can he take care of God's church?)* (NIV).

This is a hard one for many to handle. Maybe they are experiencing a short season of frustration with their child or household and they are wondering if that discounts them from continuing in service. I think that the main point of discussion should be the attitude that you tolerate. I believe that Paul is talking about tolerance. If you tolerate wrong attitudes in your home, then you will tolerate wrong attitudes in the church. If you tolerate lies and chaos at home, then you will tolerate these things on your team and in the church. I believe that it takes more skill to keep an orderly home than it does to keep an orderly church. Yet, if you can develop these skills at home, you will do well at church.

Presently, divorce rates among leaders in the Body of Christ stand at 60 percent. Over 80 percent of pastors' wives wish that their husbands would never have entered the work of the ministry, and over 22,000 pastors leave the ministry annually. Seventy percent of our pastors are plagued by depression. These stats can be changed by what we do at home.[4]

"Team Family"

Here are a few thoughts for you if you are married: keep the team mind-set at all times with your spouse and children. You cannot be the only called and anointed one in your family anymore. Even if they don't want to work directly in the ministry, they are still in the ministry as a part of your family. This is important for all of your family to understand. Your call is as a team, and you must help them understand that their lifestyle is ministry in and of itself. When you are ministering to people, they are a part of that because they allow you to do so. Always protect your family from the ministry and people who are involved in the ministry. Your first ministry is to your family, and if you never forget that, your family will enjoy being a part of the team. All are called at this point even though they may not be directly chosen to do ministry.

Your Spouse as Friend and Lover

Your spouse is your number one friend and covenant partner. If this is not the case, then I encourage you to strategically make your spouse a friend and a lover with your passion and excitement. This means that you must get started right away. If you have lost your friendship with your spouse, then you must start talking again. Open up the gates of communication; remember to listen instead of talk. I have talked to women who say that they can't talk to their husbands because they don't have anything to say.

That may be true about the subjects that you want them to talk about, but first find out what they are interested in, and you will not be able to shut them up.

An acquaintance of mine took his wife on a short-term mission trip, and they started talking about moving to the foreign country they were visiting. A week into it she said, "I am going home; I can't live by myself with you." This woman is one of the friendliest women I know; she can make a friend anywhere at any time. Back home she has a huge network of friends, but in this country she would have to learn the language in order to meet new people. She was drying up because her husband wasn't a very talkative person. He told me that he started praying for God to change his wife, and God said to him, "Your wife doesn't need to change; you do. You must learn to talk and communicate with her." He immediately started to open up the lines of communication. His wife noticed the difference and changed her mind about him and the trip to the foreign land. Someone will always need to change, and most of the time it will be you.

Make sure that you keep the romance in your relationship with your spouse and keep an eye on the level of laughter and intimacy you and your spouse experience together. A lack of either should be a red flag, and something must be done immediately. If you have more fun with people other than your spouse, there is a problem. Keep it healthy in the bedroom by having fun in the bedroom. If you don't know what your spouse enjoys, then you will need to talk and laugh about it. Sometimes we make everything so serious and boring; just have fun! Go out to dinner or do something special on a regular basis to keep variety. My wife and I are best friends; we laugh and talk all day. We travel together, and we talk on the phone the majority of the time that we are away from each other. We really have never quit the courting and honeymoon stage and we don't plan on it. Who says that you have to?

We have three children and we have to make time for each other, but it is possible if you really want to spend time together. My wife and

I enjoy watching movies together. We also enjoy a little competition in our relationship; nothing serious, but we like games like solitaire, another time it was backgammon and lately it has been 1-minute Bejeweled on Facebook. We keep fun in our relationship. We make each other laugh on purpose. Once you stop laughing together you stop doing other things together if you know what I mean. If you go to the movies every week, then it is probably getting mundane and is no longer a date night. Do something different: read a book together (*The Five Love Languages,* for instance), go on a walk, or rent a limo.[5]

Cherishing Your Family

Play often with your children. Sometimes it is hard to pull away from something that is important to go and look at the gecko, play a video game, or hide and go seek, but it must be done from time to time. I don't think that you need to give in to this every time, because your children also need to learn how to respect the ministry, yet from time to time you can show them that to you they are more important than the duties of the ministry. If they feel like they are always sacrificing and never benefiting, they will certainly resent the ministry, God, and possibly even you.

You must make it a priority to keep your family saved, healthy, and happy. Your family is your lifeline. I know ministers who have devoted their lives to ministering to others only to lose their own family. The Father didn't force His Son Jesus to go to the cross; Jesus volunteered for the job because He was a part of the *team* to get the job done. Don't unknowingly sacrifice your children for the applause of strangers or your spouse for the clamor of groupies. A great Scripture regarding this is First Timothy 5:8: *"But if any provide not for his own, and specially for those of his own house, he hath denied the faith, and is worse than an infidel"* (KJV). We always see this provision as financial, yet it also includes such things as affection, honor, hope, relaxation, love, fun, intellectual conversation, adventure, and future.

We cannot provide our best to others and not provide the same or better to our family. In addition, I should say you must provide financially for your family in an uncommon way. Let your family experience the best that life has to offer. This is the will of God, and this will be a dynamic witness to those around you. The way you provide for your family shows both your strength and your faith. Make sure that you have regular family vacations and times of leisure. Add to your schedule a Sabbath day or a day of rest. If you minister on Sundays, Sunday cannot be your day of rest. On this day of rest, train yourself to think positively all day, train yourself to spend the day as a family as best as you can, and treat yourselves to a special day in the presence of God. This day can be Monday or whatever day works for you and your family. Keep this day holy— separate it from the rest of the days. On my family day, I rarely, if ever, do any ministry work; this day is to relax and refresh with my family and my God.

You have to intentionally cherish and keep your family, win friends, and influence people. These things have to become a conviction in your heart and a way of life. This means you will have to choose to do these things. Make the choice to live a whole and healthy life with healthy relationships. Relationships should become one of the most important things for you to preserve as you grow in leading as a servant. Nurture them, and they will bear wonderful and lasting fruit.

Endnotes

1. Dale Carnegie, *How to Win Friends and Influence People* (New York, NY: Simon & Schuster, 1937, 2009).

2. "Parazeloo"; http://www.studylight.org/lex/grk/view.cgi?number=3863.

3. John C. Maxwell, *Developing the Leader Within You* (Thomas Nelson, 2000).

4. See Maranatha Life, "Life-Line For Pastors"; http://maranathalife.com/lifeline/stats.htm.

5. Gary Chapman, *The Five Love Languages* (Chicago, IL: Northfield Publishing, 1995).

CHAPTER THIRTEEN

GLORIOUS LIVING

LEADERS AND SERVERS ALIKE need to live a progressive lifestyle. It is not enough for your leader to live a progressive lifestyle; you as the follower must experience at least a portion of the same progressive grace. God has given us His increasing grace to live in God's glory. John 1:14-16 says,

> *And the Word became flesh and dwelt among us, and we beheld His glory, the glory as of the only begotten of the Father, full of grace and truth. John bore witness of Him and cried out, saying, "This was He of whom I said, 'He who comes after me is preferred before me, for He was before me.'" And of His fullness we have all received, and grace for grace.*

Of the fullness of God's glory we have received *"and grace for grace."* Notice that the passage doesn't say *from grace to grace*. You cannot increase in grace without first increasing your expectation; each new level of expectation must possess a new level of grace. Let's read it again from the Amplified version:

*And the Word (Christ) became flesh (human, incarnate) and
tabernacled (fixed His tent of flesh, lived awhile) among us;
and we [actually] saw His glory (His honor, His majesty),
such glory as an only begotten son receives from his father,
full of grace (favor, loving-kindness) and truth. John testified
about Him and cried out, This was He of Whom I said, He
Who comes after me has priority over me, for He was before
me. [He takes rank above me, for He existed before I did. He
has advanced before me, because He is my Chief.] For out
of His fullness (abundance) we have all received [all had a
share and we were all supplied with] one grace after another
and spiritual blessing upon spiritual blessing and even favor
upon favor and gift [heaped] upon gift* (John 1:14-16).

This implies that we receive one level of favor upon another level of
favor, one level of grace upon another level of grace. If this is true, we should
not continue to live according to the previous favor after we have received
the graduated level of God's grace. For example, if I have been lifting
weights every day for a year religiously, and after a year I am still lifting the
same amount of weight without testing the limits of my strength, then I am
simply cheating myself. If I truly want to grow, I must add weight to the
weight bar that I am lifting, so that I can increase in strength and capacity.
God's glory is given to us with the intention of increase and growth. If this
is true, we have received all of God's glory, and it is entrusted to us based on
the increasing growth that we possess. We increase in grace according to the
use of that grace, just as we increase our muscles according to our exercise
routine. The glory of God desires to transform us spiritually, emotionally,
mentally, physically, and financially.

In Second Corinthians 3:18, we read, *"And we, who with unveiled faces
all reflect the Lord's glory, are being transformed into His likeness with ever-
increasing glory, which comes from the Lord, who is the Spirit"* (NIV). We
should live with an understanding that God wants to glorify His name

through us. I am not talking about shining and illuminating glory, but I am talking about the Haggai 2:7-9 glory:

> *"I will shake all nations, and the desired of all nations will come, and I will fill this house with glory," says the Lord Almighty. "The silver is Mine and the gold is Mine," declares the Lord Almighty. "The glory of this present house will be greater than the glory of the former house," says the Lord Almighty. "And in this place I will grant peace," declares the Lord Almighty* (NIV).

This Scripture is a great example of increasing glory: *"The glory of this present house will be greater than the glory of the former house"* is a statement of progress. The root meaning of *glory* comes from the Hebrew word *kabad* (kaw-bad'), or *kabowd* (kaw-bode'), which means to be heavy, in a good sense (numerous, rich, honorable; causatively, to make weighty).[1] God wants our words to be increasingly weighty. God wants our finances to increase unto wealth and riches. God wants our name to increase in honor and respect, and to have more influence next year than we did this year. *Kabad* never stays the same; it demands that we grow. It is the same as the Kingdom of God. The Kingdom of God never ends, never retreats, never stays the same, and never stops growing. We have the glorious Kingdom of God within us, manifesting God's glory around us—not just with signs and wonders, but with influence. In Haggai, the glory of God referred to silver and gold. The splendor of God was material and tangible. The glory of God should be seen by our neighbors to the point that they call us blessed—meaning "to be envied." There should be so much glory or love in my marriage that the un-churched look at my marriage and become envious; they should see my lifestyle and become envious. Second Corinthians 8:19-21 says,

> *and not only that, but who was also chosen by the churches to travel with us with this gift, which is administered by us to the glory of the Lord Himself and to show your*

ready mind, avoiding this: that anyone should blame us in this lavish gift which is administered by us—providing honorable things, not only in the sight of the Lord, but also in the sight of men.

The glory of God should provide honorable things in the sight of God and man. God wants men to see our prospering; God wants us to show His goodness to the world.

How does this translate to leadership? Let's look at Proverbs 14:28: *"In a multitude of people is a king's honor, but in the lack of people is the downfall of a prince."* The honor of leadership is that someone is following. The glory and honor of a master is that multitudes follow. It is no good to be a self-proclaimed leader having no followers. Leadership doesn't exist without followers. I have seen many people with the title of leader, and yet they have no one following. In fact, these individuals were not leaders at all, but managers. There is nothing wrong with management, but management is not leadership. Leadership is a frontline position and demands constant change, increase, and new vision. If a person who has a leadership position does not influence people to themselves, they will experience downfall because of the lack of people following. Show forth the glory of God by first being a dynamic follower, and then metamorphose into leadership by attracting followers. This is the glory of God manifesting in the life of a servant: ever-increasing grace, ever-increasing glory, ever-increasing levels, ever-increasing honor, ever-increasing wealth, ever-increasing followership, and ever-increasing leadership.

Endnote

1. "Kabad"; http://www.studylight.org/lex/heb/view.cgi?number=03513; "Kabowd"; http://www.studylight.org/lex/heb/view.cgi?number=03519.

PART 4

FOLLOW the LEADER

CHAPTER FOURTEEN

FOLLOW ME

I WAS WATCHING MY sons and one of their friends play one day, and they happened to be playing "follow the leader." One shouted, "Let's play follow the leader!" and the others quickly ran to that one and began to mimic what he was doing. They walked where he walked; they made the same moves that he made. It was fun to watch because I had forgotten about that game. I think everybody at one time or another has played "follow the leader." I immediately thought how great it would be if people jumped into the work of the ministry to be trained, following the leader's enthusiasm.

Paul wanted his followers to mimic him even as he followed Christ. In First Corinthians 11:1, Paul wrote, "*Follow my example, as I follow the example of Christ*" (NIV). This statement doesn't seem to have the same effect on adults as it does children. Yet, Jesus challenged His disciples to become like little children in their faith. I think that we often have such cynicism and skepticism that we can't follow with the same pure heart and fun-loving joy as a child would. Like children, we should believe that the best is yet to come and anticipate what challenging and exciting move may come next from the leader we are following. This is the game of Follow the Leader. Somehow it changes once you get to a certain age. Maybe, because we have been so challenged to be independent and in control, we have lost the art of followership.

The Art of Followership

The Scripture says in Habakkuk 2:2, *"Write the vision and make it plain on tablets, that he may run who reads it."* We have people who see the vision and compare it with their notes to see if they agree or not. If they had a chisel, they would try to make it better fit their lifestyle. In the biblical culture, people knew what it meant to follow. In our western society, we don't understand the culture of following. Actually, in the biblical culture it was a privilege to be asked to follow. All of those whom Jesus called were rejects who were not called to follow a rabbi, so they had to go work in the family business and apprentice under their father or family members. Jesus gave them dignity by asking them to follow Him.

In our western culture, we have been taught that if you are not the lead man, you are not as important and lack something. So we have many people who would be better used if they linked their gifts and talents with someone who is better suited for the driver's seat. Some drivers don't know how to read maps or follow directions well; others don't know how to drive properly, yet they can decipher a map well and have great directional skills. They would be productive if they joined forces and learned to serve one another, instead of being out of rank and ineffective. We need people who can see a vision and let it resonate within them, then take off running with the vision burning in their hearts, no matter what part of the vision they are called to serve in.

Own the Vision

The first part of followership is to own the vision. If you can't own the vision, you will never run. If you are serving in a ministry and you are not sure of the vision, ask about it and work hard on your part to gain clarity. Your leader needs you to be able to take off running with all of your heart, working to bring the vision to pass. If the vision doesn't live in you, then the vision won't live in any of the people who serve with you. You have to first be able to articulate the vision as you pass it down to those who serve on your team. The moment the vision stops moving through the team, growth stops, and the vision starts to get diluted. Own the vision, and then begin running. You must make sure that you are an attractive leader-servant as you begin to run because people are going to relate to *your leader* by the way *you* serve and lead. Make sure that you don't have anything in your life that will distract others from running and participating with the vision.

Your goal must become, "follow me as I follow my leader who is following Christ." This is called duplication. Duplicate yourself in those who follow you. When I was a youth pastor, it was my job to make sure that the vision, culture, and values of the youth ministry represented the vision, culture, and values of the church as a whole. Yet the youth didn't really connect with the main church. They related to me because my job was to develop them into followers of Christ as they followed me as I followed the lead pastor. We designed a leadership track for those who wanted to become disciples of Christ. This 90-day discipleship track was simple. We gave them a different book every month, a schedule of scriptures that needed to be read or memorized, and an essay to be written on each book and the scriptures. They also needed to fast from food and television every Wednesday for the 90 days. Nor could they could go to the movies during those 16 weeks. They also sat in the front and took notes in service and turned in their notebooks of all the progress every week. By the end of the

90 days, they were thanking us for developing them into disciples of Christ. The truth is that all we did was give them a system and accountability; they did all of the work.

Another thing that I adopted as a youth pastor is to never do anything alone. I always involved a student in what I did. I didn't do all of this for my sake, but I did it for the sake of the vision, culture, and values of the leader of the house. Wherever the vision, culture, and values stop flowing to the next level of people in an organizational chart is where the growth stops. For example, I used to live in San Diego, just around the corner from Skyline Church, where John Maxwell was the pastor. One day I was at the gas station next to the church, and a gentleman at the pump next to me and I started talking. The conversation led to the understanding that he attended Skyline. I asked him, "What is the vision of the church?" I will never forget the response of this man. As a parishioner, he knew the vision for the church verbatim. I realized that Skyline church had such a strong leadership culture that the vision statement seeped down to this man's level. Make sure that your team members have read and captured the vision, that they truly own and run in the vision, as they activate their gifts and talents for the work.

At this point, you are a living example to those who are following you. If you don't have anyone following you, then I suggest that you discover ways to make yourself more attractive, and that starts with going back to the vision. Ask yourself, "Am I a complete representation of the vision? Can people see me and know the direction of the church? Am I the essence of the culture of the church or organization? Do I live like my leader, do I sound like my leader, and do I express the same character qualities and passion as my leader?" These questions simply boil down to one powerful question: "Am I following my leader as I should be?" This question should be asked often if you really don't have a personal agenda for serving the leader and the organization. Your place in the organization has nothing to do with you; it is about the vision of the organization and the Kingdom.

We must learn to remove our personal agendas for the sake of winning, training, and sending.

The Nike Way

Running is reading the vision and moving. You should know when God has answered your prayers and you have felt the internal excitement. Reading a vision is a call to action. The world will outdo us as long as we keep waiting. Every second that passes another soul perishes; we must be about our Father's business. Believe me, if you are going the wrong direction, God will show you. Most people who have made big mistakes in life have made them because of disobedience. They didn't have the inner excitement or the inner peace. I am not encouraging foolishness. I think that we should learn to pray as we move forward. I heard something years ago, and I believe that it is a good way to live: "Pray like it is up to God and work like it is up to you." Religiosity wants us to stand around and wait until an angel appears or a sign in the heavens manifests before we get moving. I say, "Take action now!" Action is the key to results. If you don't take positive and progressive action, you are still taking action by doing nothing, which is recession. Follow the Nike way: "Just do it!" Paul says it this way: *"The things which you learned and received and heard and saw in me, these do, and the God of peace will be with you"* (Phil. 4:9). These things do!

As a Christian who has been engrafted into Christ, I believe that if something is going to be done, it is going be done through us, the engrafted. So what are we waiting for? Habakkuk 2:3 says, *"For the vision is yet for an appointed time; but at the end it will speak, and it will not lie. Though it tarries, wait for it; because it will surely come, it will not tarry."* This verse still doesn't give the freedom of sitting and waiting. It actually gives the implication that you should never give up. It suggests that you should wrap yourself up in the vision as you continue to pursue it, become a person of action, and learn to take action.

In 2002, I received an idea of a new marketing product while walking through the Dallas airport. I had made the decision earlier that year to pursue whatever invention idea I received, no mater how wild it sounded. I made an appointment with an invention attorney and found that it was a viable idea. So step-by-step I worked on this product. It took seven years for this product to finally get patented and find its entrance into a market. Some of this time, I was waiting, other times I was questioning whether it was worth the effort, and other times were full of joy. I never stopped because I vowed that I was going to chase it down until I absolutely exhausted the options. When you have an idea, take action. When I have a new idea, I chase it down with the mind-set that I am either going to prove that it will work or prove that it will not work. It is never acceptable to assume that it will not work.

Covering Your Leader

Often people who are serving leaders don't understand that their leaders are going to be changing and developing right in front of their eyes. Leaders don't have the privilege of stepping out of the glass house in order to metamorphose into the great leader whom they becoming. Sometimes they will be processing the next level of the vision, or waiting on clarity as they are casting vision for the next level. If you can protect and flex with your leader through these times, you will be rewarded for your loyalty. The worst thing that you could do to your leader is to uncover them in a vulnerable time. This caused God to fight against Noah's sons in the Bible:

> *Ham, the father of Canaan, saw his father's nakedness and told his two brothers outside. But Shem and Japheth took a garment and laid it across their shoulders; then they walked in backward and covered their father's nakedness. Their faces were turned the other way so that they would*

not see their father's nakedness. When Noah awoke from his wine and found out what his youngest son had done to him, he said, "Cursed be Canaan! The lowest of slaves will he be to his brothers." He also said, "Blessed be the Lord, the God of Shem! May Canaan be the slave of Shem. May God extend the territory of Japheth; may Japheth live in the tents of Shem, and may Canaan be his slave" (Genesis 9:22-27 NIV).

A curse was placed on the son who didn't properly handle his father's nakedness.

Always cover your leader. Never let your leader feel naked or embarrassed by pointing out their flaws or even joking about your leader's weaknesses or flaws. The people who understand their leader the most are those who frame their relationship in submission, humility, and prayer. Prayer will help you understand what is taking place. During these transitions, a prayerful servant will not focus on weakness, but will see what is ahead. Great leaders and followers will have to develop foresight. Without this foresight, present circumstances will be misjudged. Remember, God works on your leader the same way that He works on you. Don't be impatient with transitions; there are so many things that take place during times of growth. God is dealing with you; He is also dealing with your leader, and He is dealing with the members of the organization. God is dealing with your leader as your leader is dealing with the staff, the business affairs of the organization, personal life, and family. These transitional times are when you should pick up the load as much as you can to help with the morale and comfort of your leader. Foresight will help you keep from despising the day of small things. God has an amazing way of fine-tuning things and causing the end to be better than the beginning.

It was this understanding about God's heart that caused my wife and I to take on a church that was located in the worst area of Seattle, with a history of frequent pastoral turnovers over a 70-year history. The church was two weeks from losing its property, and the congregation didn't know that they were simply a few weeks from losing their church home and investments. Debts were mounting and many of the congregation left the day that we showed up. The monthly income was about $6,000 and the mortgage alone was $5,900. At the same time, we had several other opportunities that at face value seemed much better options. But this thought—that God wants everything that He starts to finish well—pushed us to move forward with confidence that God could use us to pull this church out.

My wife and I had been traveling in ministry for years together. We believe that we are a team and that a team shouldn't be split up. We traveled three weeks out of the month around the world. So if we were going to take on this church, it would have to take care of our personal needs. God, being the greatest turnaround King, turned it around. In just a few weeks, the finances tripled, we stopped the foreclosure, the congregation immediately grew, and our salary needs were met.

If you are planning to take on a chaotic situation, it is a necessity that you realize that God is a turnaround King and that He wants everything that He starts to finish well. I have had several of the previous pastors stop by and see what we are now doing and say, "This is exactly what we saw. It is the vision that this church was started with 70 years ago." God wants everything that we do to finish strong. From creation until now everything has a seed. Everything that God does starts with a seed and grows into something that is better and greater than the seed. If this is true for the ministry you serve, then you must learn to see what is coming ahead.

Adjusting to a leader who is changing and growing in authority takes maturity. Keep the vision in front of you and keep speaking the vision, especially to those who may gripe to you in private. If you have lost the vision and can't seem to get it back, it is better for you to move on before you find yourself living in resentment and complaining, which will ultimately lead to negative and dangerous repercussions. The moment you gossip against your leader or the organization, no matter how justified or right you think that you are, you will be wrong. You set yourself up as an enemy of God and His servants, and ultimately you will be judged by God for it (see Rom. 13:1-5). To allow backbiting or gossip to enter into your ears by others is sin. Guard your heart, for from your heart flows the issues of life (see Prov. 4:23). Recapture the vision and heart of your leader if you can; if you cannot, then you must set up an exit strategy that will not damage the organization or the Kingdom of God in any way. Follow with excellence as you build the Kingdom of God.

Confrontation

Confrontation is a part of leadership. A culture void of confrontation is a culture void of boundaries and accountability, which is a culture void of positive results.

There are several reasons why a leader may choose not to confront, the first being that he or she is frightened of how the person may respond. The fear of rejection is a killer of the leader's credibility. Second, he or she may think that confrontation is mean. Both of these reasons come from an unhealthy mind-set about confrontation. We should think of confrontation as something that helps the person being confronted to become a better person and better at working in the organization. If she is the right person for the job, she will desire to do a better job. We must confront her for the sake of the vision of the organization and the mission of the Kingdom. We must confront and tell the truth, only in love, as the Bible says.

The Bible is full of great pictures of confrontation. Think about when Jesus was speaking to His disciples at the Lord's Supper: He pulled out an apron and a pan of water and washed His disciples' feet (see John 13:5). You don't have to literally wash your staff's feet while confronting them, but you should have the heart of a foot washer, the heart of a servant. If you have been under a cruel leader (I call them "Saul leaders"), you may think that you must tell people off or bluntly attack everything that is wrong. This form of hard leadership is abusive. Most people will revert back to the wrong way of things once they are no longer under that kind of leadership; in the end, they will not sustain long-term change. Ask yourself this question, "Am I trying to simply get the job done, or do I want to make this person a better person, a better follower, and ultimately a better leader?"

So often I confront by setting a good example or expectation. When I have team members who are living beneath their potential or beneath the call and culture of the organization, I need to help them raise their expectation. I don't sit them down and tell them off. We sit down with them and talk through their passion and vision. Once we get on the same page of what the ultimate purpose looks like, we then find out if they are open to hear what is holding them back from that passionate vision. We take a coaching approach, not a dictator approach. As a coach, I want to tell the truth in love. As a coach, I must give them the tools necessary for their success. Showing people what is possible is one of the most powerful forms of confrontation. Set their personal achievement levels high and encourage them to reach higher. Always tell the truth in love as you cast vision. If they are not motivated by this kind of encouragement, then you have a larger problem than simply confronting them. You have the wrong person in place and must quickly move them laterally (or out) so that they can prosper where they are motivated. You have to be willing to be a coach, not simply a commander.

Conflict or confrontation should not be about telling people what to do or what they are doing wrong; it is about helping people think better and make better choices. Leadership helps people become better thinkers and executers of higher-level thinking.

Proper confrontation is helping people come to a conclusion on their own. The true goal of confrontation is to get the person that you are helping to realize their shortcomings, while giving them inspiration to carry on with dignity and confidence. People should walk away encouraged and ready for the job after they have been confronted. They should have a greater efficacy level. This doesn't mean that there will not be repercussions. Most of the time there will be some form of repercussion. If done with love and mercy, the repercussion will be seen as the price that must be paid for credibility, and not as a punishment. Once the confrontation is over, it is finished. I don't want failure looming over my team; that will bring about performance anxiety.

I like the way Jesus confronted people. Let's look at a few. When Peter was lovingly trying to give Jesus some heartfelt and truly caring advice, he slipped into mediocrity and forgot the big picture: that the Son of Man must die. Jesus understood that Peter's mediocrity was something more than bad thinking. It was an inspired bad thought from the devil. He said, *"Get behind Me, Satan!"* (Matt. 16:23). Jesus attacked the unseen issues in Peter's life and separated them from Peter as a person. Jesus knew that Peter could not be influenced by the devil in the future if Peter was to become the rock of the Church.

What about when the Sons of Thunder wanted to call down fire from Heaven to consume people? Jesus' rebuke was simply a reminder of who they were. He said, "Do you not know who your father is?" (see Luke 9:54-55). This is an incredible picture of a leader who really wants the best for his team. Pray for them before you confront or rebuke, and pray for them and affirm them after you rebuke.

You don't have to be a hard leader to confront. You are not a loving leader if you don't confront. Find your style, line it up with Jesus' style, and use it. There are skills that come into play, but most of the time it is love that speaks the loudest. If you find yourself lacking love, increase your prayer for the individual before you confront.

Bill Hybels says that vision leaks. Most of the time, people need to be reminded of who they are, the vision, and the part that they are expected to play in achieving that vision.

Other times you will have to confront more than performance. You will have to confront outright sin. Nathan the prophet had a great strategy in dealing with David, not only to let David know the severity of his sin, but to get him to repent for missing the mark.

> And the Lord sent Nathan unto David. And he came unto him, and said unto him, There were two men in one city; the one rich, and the other poor. The rich man had exceeding many flocks and herds: but the poor man had nothing, save one little ewe lamb, which he had bought and nourished up: and it grew up together with him, and with his children; it did eat of his own morsel, and drank of his own cup, and lay in his bosom, and was unto him as a daughter. And there came a traveler unto the rich man, and he spared to take of his own flock and of his own herd, to dress for the wayfaring man that was come unto him, but took the poor man's lamb, and dressed it for the man that was come to him. And David's anger was greatly kindled against the man; and he said to Nathan, As the Lord liveth, the man that hath done this is worthy to die: and he shall restore the lamb fourfold, because he did this thing, and because he had no pity. And Nathan said to David, Thou art the man (2 Samuel 12:1-7 NJV).

Nathan built a rapport with King David and told him a story that would make the imagery stick. The prophet used wisdom to confront. He didn't go straight to the point or the issue. The use of wisdom caused David to come to the conclusion on his own. Nathan also discovered that King

David had not completely lost his mind, because he was able to recognize right and wrong. Nathan made sure of that first. Sometimes people form their own reality so strongly that no matter what you say, they will stick to their own deception. It is much harder to get a person on common ground once you have confronted him or her. It is much more effective to develop rapport and build a common understanding. Once everybody is on neutral and common ground and clear thinking has been established, then your job of confrontation will be easier. Nathan had done such an outstanding job in building the imagery that David was flaming hot for justice and all he had to say was, "You are that man." The punishment that David had exacted for the other man was due him, yet God had more mercy than David. Remember that lesson: God will most likely have more mercy than you could ever muster up. Seek God's Word and counsel to find God's heart in confronting, all the while keeping the culture and standards of the organization. Usually God's mercy and God's justice go hand in hand.

Work on becoming a better storyteller and vision caster. These skills will help tremendously in confronting those that you lead. The power of anger and harshness wears thin and hampers performance. Ultimately, you want the people you are confronting to be better off after you confront them than they were before.

Lasting change can only occur when a person has an "aha! moment"—a moment of inspiration and revelation. Inspire your team at all times, even when you are confronting them to keep away from sin, or to achieve the deadline, or to overcome mediocrity.

CHAPTER FIFTEEN

MINISTRY vs. LEADERSHIP

FOLLOWING IS THE CORNERSTONE of leadership: a person void of followers is really not a leader. Anywhere the culture of leadership is being developed, you will also find a strong understanding of submission, training, and serving. When I first began to lose some of the leaders who had moved from their homes—quitting jobs and selling businesses—in order to help us build the church, I wondered what happened. With lots of prayer and heart searching, the Lord provided me with an understanding of followership. Actually, it was when I began to preach a sermon on followership in our church that I first began to lose some of our key leaders. I had been working hard to establish this culture in our church and amongst our team and realized that the proper heart of submission was not present to handle such a message. I didn't set this culture from the get-go, so it was hard to turn the present direction in our leadership. I was puzzled because we had always had a strong and prospering ministry. My wife and I, along with our children, had traveled extensively throughout the world.

We saw many miracles and lives changed. We had a great track record of character and purity, but I just couldn't figure out the problem. It took over twenty leaders and workers leaving before I really began to seek God for understanding.

I felt like God wanted to show me something about Jesus and His ministry. So I started reading the New Testament again starting with Matthew. The first thing that I noticed was that Jesus handpicked His first four followers. We see this in Matthew 4:18-22:

> *As Jesus was walking beside the Sea of Galilee, He saw two brothers, Simon called Peter and his brother Andrew. They were casting a net into the lake, for they were fishermen. "Come, follow Me," Jesus said, "and I will make you fishers of men." At once they left their nets and followed Him. Going on from there, He saw two other brothers, James son of Zebedee and his brother John. They were in a boat with their father Zebedee, preparing their nets. Jesus called them, and immediately they left the boat and their father and followed Him* (NIV).

I also noticed that these men were busy working and were already active achievers. They were not looking for an opportunity. A long time ago I heard a businessman say that the best people to hire or to recruit are busy people, because busy people already have the skills of managing their life and time. If you want to recruit someone who has a lot of time, you must first ask yourself, "Why do they have so much available time?"

The next thing I observed was that Jesus called them and they immediately followed. Even though they were working with their father, they left him without a question. I don't remember their father ever coming back up. I love when people are decisive. Followers need to be decisive and committed. Successful people don't take a lot of time making decisions; they usually can make a quick decision once they have all of the facts.

As I reached the end of chapter 4 and began reading chapter 5, I spotted something that I had never seen before in this beatitudes chapter:

> *Large crowds from Galilee, the Decapolis, Jerusalem, Judea and the region across the Jordan followed Him. Now when He saw the crowds, He went up on a mountainside and sat down. His disciples came to Him, and He began to teach them* (Matthew 4:25; 5:1 NIV).

From this passage, we see that Jesus had two groups following Him, each for different reasons, expecting different things. One group was the crowd who followed Jesus because of His *ministry*—what He could do for them, and how He could meet their needs. The other group was His disciples who followed because of His *leadership*. Jesus handpicked His disciples before they ever knew His ministry. So they followed because they knew He was a leader; they received His leadership. The crowd came later after the ministry of Jesus was seen. The thing that I immediately learned is that the people on my team had followed me because of my ministry and not because of my leadership. Yet once they had joined our ministry, and I started trying to direct them as a leader and not as a minister, I was no longer giving them what they expected, and they got frustrated. Jesus knew that the crowd could not follow the leader; they were only prepared to follow the minister.

I was always taught to gather your leaders and the crowd would come. According to Jesus' style of ministry building, He recruited four and put His culture within them, then began to minister to the community and drew a crowd. As the crowd grew, Jesus added more disciples. We see how He did that in verse 1: *"Now when He saw the crowds, He went up on a mountainside and sat down. His disciples came to Him"* (Matt. 5:1 NIV). As a builder, I look at this scripture a little differently. First, the Bible usually clearly makes a distinction between the multitude and a gathering of his disciples. If you read the Scriptures with a leadership lens, you begin to look for that distinction. Leaders understand that what you say to the multitude is very different to what you say to the builders behind closed doors. Jesus' number of disciples grew each day. Jesus' ministry grew each day. We must remember that Jesus started with four disciples and then he added more, which eventually became the 12 Apostles. Then Jesus appointed another 70 as His disciples. So we can see that Jesus was a developer of leader-followers and not just a communicator to the multitude. Jesus' discipleship actually became a small crowd. If you pay close attention you can see that there's a strong dividing line between the multitude and a mass of disciples.

As I look at Matthew 5:1, I recognized a few important things. The first thing that we must see is how Jesus postured himself. Any public speaker should know that if you are going to communicate to a large crowd, let's say a multitude without any form of amplification, you would need to physically stand in order to project. The fact that Jesus was sitting shows me that He was about to address a smaller crowd than a multitude. Whenever Jesus addressed the multitude, He postured Himself physically, or sat at least one time in a way that was very strategic. He was teaching, and the crowd grew to a multitude on the seashore, and then Jesus moved into a boat and sat to address the multitude. It clearly says *a multitude* in Matthew 13:2 (KJV). Water can actually act as an amplifier of sound. It is possible that Jesus moved into the boat to amplify His voice because His crowd increased from a smaller group into a larger group. In Matthew 5:1, it is clear that Jesus started His communication to His disciples. Who knows the number of disciples? It could have been 4, 12, 70, 120, or more. In our ministry, there is a huge difference between those who are followers of our leadership and those who are followers of our ministry. The same is true here with Jesus. There is a huge difference between those who followed Jesus as disciples and those who followed Jesus as those who needed a miracle or forgiveness.

A disciple is one who wants to become like their teacher. A follower of miracles needs a miracle and may never actually become a disciple. If you think about it, how many of the twelve apostles came from a ministry experience, where Jesus healed them and then they followed Him because He was their Healer? The original 12 didn't get healed or delivered from demons by Jesus, but they were redirected by Jesus. They weren't living a purpose-driven life and Jesus came into their lives to lead them into purpose. They followed Jesus the leader and not Jesus the miracle worker. Jesus didn't do one miracle to get their attention, He simply said, "Follow me!" and they all left home and/or careers to do so. I myself realized that those who followed me because I could do miracles were less reliable followers than those who followed me because I redirected their lives as a leader. The multitude yelled, "Crucify Him!", but when it was all said and done, it was those who believed in His leadership that showed up in the upper room on the day of Pentecost.

This brings me to my next thought regarding this leadership moment. In modern times we do leadership retreats, sometimes called advances. We do leadership conferences. It is sad that we usually only see Jesus as a minister and not as a leader with thousands of followers. We know that Jesus was accustomed to separating Himself from the multitudes to a place of solace. Wouldn't it make sense that He would have a time to pull together the larger group of those who followed His leadership? The second thing that we can learn from this passage is that Jesus pulled away with His disciples: *"His disciples came to Him."* We conduct miracle services, wealth building seminars and conferences, and we do leadership conferences and services. A person who comes to our leadership meetings expecting a miracle may be very disappointed when they leave. They may actually get a miracle when they ask for prayer, but we will not focus on miracles in that meeting setting. At leadership events, the teaching will surround leadership and building of teams.

I have read the Gospel over and over looking at it with a leadership lens, and the more I look, the more I notice that the Bible shows Jesus pulling His team aside and giving them a different insight than the crowd had available to them. At one point, Jesus told His disciples that it was for them to know the mysteries of His teachings but not for the larger group. The funny thing is that the disciples were just as confused as the larger crowd by His teaching.

> *And He said to them, He who has ears to hear, let him hear. And when He was alone, they who were about Him, with the Twelve, asked Him concerning the parable. And He said to them, To you it is given to know the mystery of the kingdom of God. But to those outside, all these things are given in parables so that seeing they may see, and not perceive; and hearing they may hear, and not understand; lest at any time they should be converted, and their sins should be forgiven them. And He said to them, Do you not know this parable? And how then will you know all parables?* (Mark 4:9-13 MKJV)

What was He saying to them? He was telling them that they had the privilege of hearing Him address the crowd and that they could enter into private quarters, ask questions about it and get answers because they were followers of His leadership and not just followers of His ministry. Jesus also used parables to challenge His followers to probe deeper for answers. "*And He said to them, Do you not know this parable? And how then will you know all parables?*" (Mark 4:13 MKJV) Good leaders don't teach by telling their followers what to do or even how to do it. But good leaders teach by asking questions and by causing their followers to ask probing questions. There is a dynamic book titled *Quiet Leadership* which has great tools on the how's and why's of developing this style of leadership. *Quiet Leadership* author David Rock says, "The first step to being a Quiet Leader is to think about people's thinking. In other words, to become passionate about improving not *what* people are thinking about, but the *way* they think."

We think that love makes everything easy. Love makes everything worth the effort. Love adds value. Jesus didn't want people who had little interest in becoming followers of His leadership to follow Him into salvation. We know this by His own words: *"lest at any time they should be converted, and their sins should be forgiven them."* We know that Jesus came with the mandate to save all mankind, but not without everyone giving up their lives nor on their own terms. Everyone who follows Christ must want more than His words and His miracles; they must also want His leadership. In Matthew 5:1, Jesus didn't handpick followers as He did with the original twelve, but He allowed the culture and momentum, which He established in the other disciples, to attract the new group of disciples. Jesus went to the mountain and sat down, waiting to see who would follow. His disciples knew that they must follow; they didn't have the choice of staying behind with the crowd. Jesus, knowing that His ministry was growing, needed to develop more leaders to handle the growth, not the other way around. The crowd stayed at the bottom of the hill, but those who wanted more than ministry took the initiative to get close to the Leader and His leadership. Those who only wanted ministry waited for the Minister to return. Once Jesus sat down, He began to teach the beatitudes, not to the crowd, but to the followers.

In our ministry, we move people from the crowd through a leadership pipeline into being a vital part of the team. The pipeline is designed to take people from the crowd and introduce them to the vision, culture, and values of the organization, to reveal to them how we can build the kingdom together as we teach them. We also have monthly leadership training meetings that are available to those who want to be developed in the culture of leadership. We have developed a leadership internship that focuses on building spiritual leaders, leaders with a prosperous soul, and leaders of organizations, by training them in what we call CEO training. All of these things are a part of our pipeline to develop leaders that will change the world. Preaching to the crowd and separating the cream from the crowd was Jesus' leadership pipeline. Each time He separated Himself, He expected someone new to follow. Followers always get a little more than the crowd does. The crowd may get the miracles, but the followers get empowered for miracles! At this stage of His ministry, Jesus stepped away to see who was with Him. This only works once the ministry has gathered a crowd.

Again we see in Matthew 9:35-38 Jesus using His pipeline method to develop a greater level in His team. This time, He is not just separating to call more followers, but He is separating in order to give His followers a greater leadership position and power.

> *And Jesus went about all the cities and villages, teaching in their synagogues, and preaching the gospel of the kingdom, and healing every sickness and every disease among the people. But when he saw the multitudes, he was moved with compassion on them, because they fainted, and were scattered abroad, as sheep having no shepherd. Then saith he unto his disciples, The harvest truly is plenteous, but the labourers are few; Pray ye therefore the Lord of the harvest, that he will send forth labourers into his harvest.* (KJV)

Jesus instructed His disciples to pray for laborers. This new focus would shift their thoughts from simply being followers to expecting followers. Every leader will need to develop leaders who can recruit and build teams. Team development is the bloodline of every organization. If Jesus didn't take this step to develop a spirit of teambuilding within His own team, it could have been devastating to the cause, especially since Jesus knew that He was going to leave the work in their hands. One of the hardest parts of building a followership culture is to keep every individual building a team around them. I even expect my personal assistant to develop a team around her so that she can delegate some of the work that is on her plate to other followers.

Jesus continues His training in Matthew 10:

> *And when he had called unto him his twelve disciples, he gave them power against unclean spirits, to cast them*

out, and to heal all manner of sickness and all manner of disease. Now the names of the twelve apostles are these; The first, Simon, who is called Peter, and Andrew his brother; James the son of Zebedee, and John his brother; Philip, and Bartholomew; Thomas, and Matthew the publican; James the son of Alphaeus, and Lebbaeus, whose surname was Thaddaeus; Simon the Canaanite, and Judas Iscariot, who also betrayed him. These twelve Jesus sent forth, and commanded them, saying, Go not into the way of the Gentiles, and into any city of the Samaritans enter ye not: But go rather to the lost sheep of the house of Israel. And as ye go, preach, saying, The kingdom of heaven is at hand. Heal the sick, cleanse the lepers, raise the dead, cast out devils: freely ye have received, freely give (Matthew 10:1-8).

Leadership and followership is about developing ways to separate people to their next level by position, doing so personally, spiritually, organizationally, and authoritatively. The best tool for developing these people is your leadership pipeline.

There is a point when the people who are following because of the ministry must make a mental discernment between wanting to be ministered to and wanting to be developed. If this paradigm shift doesn't happen, then they will grow discouraged without knowing what the problem really is. They will say that they just don't get fed, or that you aren't spiritual enough. They will begin to look for reasons why they feel the way they feel. What really needs to happen is for them to be renewed in the spirit of their mind to follow the leadership and not simply the ministry. Follow leadership, not ministry. Following ministry is an entry-level mind-set. We all must follow ministry at the outset, but once we are free and healthy, we must think growth, followership, and leadership.

Again we see in Matthew 8:18-22 that Jesus leaves the crowd to gather more disciples, and a scribe decides to follow Him:

And when Jesus saw great multitudes about Him, He gave a command to depart to the other side. Then a certain scribe came and said to Him, "Teacher, I will follow You wherever You go." And Jesus said to him, "Foxes have holes and birds of the air have nests, but the Son of Man has nowhere to lay His head." Then another of His disciples said to Him, "Lord, let me first go and bury my father." But Jesus said to him, "Follow Me, and let the dead bury their own dead."

Jesus didn't make it easy for those who wanted to join Him. After someone devotes the rest of his life to Christ, all He says to this person was that He has nowhere to lay His head. If we read between the lines we hear, "I don't have a home and neither will you if you follow Me. Are you sure you still want to follow Me?" Still another new recruit pledges to serve after he is done burying his father. I love what the *Matthew Henry Commentary* has to say about this account; it will strengthen my interpretation:

The excuse that this disciple made, to defer an immediate attendance on Christ (*v.* 21); "*Lord, suffer me first to go and bury my father.* Before I come to be a close and constant follower of thee, let me be allowed to perform this last office of respect to my father; and in the mean time, let it suffice to be a hearer of thee now and then, when I can spare time." His father (some think) was now sick, or dying, or dead; others think, he was only aged, and not likely in a course of nature, to continue long; and he desired leave to attend upon him in his sickness, at his death, and to his grave, and then he would be at Christ's service. This seemed a reasonable request, and yet it was not right. He had not the zeal he should have had for the work, and therefore pleaded this, because it seemed a plausible plea. Note, An unwilling mind never wants an excuse. The meaning of *Non vacat* is, *Non placet--The want of leisure is the want of inclination.* We will suppose it to come from a true filial affection and respect for his father, yet still the preference should have been given to Christ. Note, Many are hindered *from* and *in* the way of serious godliness, by an over-concern for their families and relations; these lawful things undo us all, and our duty to God is neglected, and postponed, under colour of discharging our debts to the world; here therefore we have need to double our guard.

In my understanding of the intention of Jesus, He basically says that if you are serious, you will let someone else bury your father and follow Me even though you are concerned for your father or your inheritance. We must be willing to leave everything to follow Christ. This guy didn't ask to go on vacation. This possibly was the last time that he would see his father; yet, if he was serious about following Christ's leadership, he must not return home. Jesus forced big, unreasonable, and sometimes unacceptable decisions on those who desired to follow His leadership. He is the same today, and we should not shy away from expecting unreasonable commitment to the Kingdom of God.

Jesus also tested the development of His followers:

> *Now when He got into a boat, His disciples followed Him. And suddenly a great tempest arose on the sea, so that the boat was covered with the waves. But He was asleep. Then His disciples came to Him and awoke Him, saying, "Lord, save us! We are perishing!" But He said to them, "Why are you fearful, O you of little faith?" Then He arose and rebuked the winds and the sea, and there was a great calm. So the men marveled, saying, "Who can this be, that even the winds and the sea obey Him? (Matthew 8:23-27)*

After the disciples entered the boat, they were hit with a storm which caused them to be uneasy and concerned about their safety. Jesus seemingly was the only one who was not concerned. I suspect that Jesus and the Father planned this little test of faith. Why? Because each leader must be tested in order to determine their progress. We should get in the habit of expecting to be tested and to test people for training purposes to discover whether or not they are growing spiritually, emotionally, and as leaders. We do this in several ways. The first is that we encourage each to submit to a written evaluation or to sit with us for a productivity review. The second thing is that we give people opportunities within a 90-day window to see how they handle a new opportunity and to test if they are teachable. We don't test for the sake of trying to trip people up; we test for the sake of evaluating their well-being and the possibility of promotion. The disciples had been with Jesus long enough that they should have been able to take care of the waves themselves.

If a follower has made the transition from following the minister to following the leader, he or she desires to emulate the leader, hoping eventually to be able to do the same as their leader. If followers are not emulating their leader, they are not growing in leadership. Emulation is a vital part in perpetuating any organization. It is called succession planning. A disciple of Christ may now be defined as one who believes His doctrine, rests upon His sacrifice, imbibes His spirit, and imitates His example.

Jesus was hoping that His disciples wanted to imitate His example, imitate His authority, and imitate His boldness. Testing will help every leader understand the developmental stages of those who are following them.

Just to confirm the pattern of growth, Jesus pulled away from His disciples. Let's look at John 6:2-3:

> ...and a great crowd of people followed Him because they saw the miraculous signs He had performed on the sick. Then Jesus went up on a mountainside and sat down with His disciples (NIV).

The beauty of followership and discipleship is that those who choose to submit to someone else receive uncommon teaching and uncommon rewards. The word that the multitude heard was different from the words that the disciples were taught. There are special blessings for those who receive the teachings in an uncommon way. We see a great example of this when the crowd hears the parables, and the disciples gain a greater clarity while sitting at the feet of the teacher.

> *Again Jesus began to teach by the lake. The crowd that gathered around Him was so large that He got into a boat and sat in it out on the lake, while all the people were along the shore at the water's edge. He taught them many things by parables, and in His teaching said: "Listen! A farmer went out to sow his seed. As he was scattering the seed, some fell along the path, and the birds came and ate it up. Some fell on rocky places, where it did not have much soil. It sprang up quickly, because the soil was shallow. But when the sun came up, the plants were scorched, and they withered because they had no root. Other seed fell among thorns, which grew up and choked the plants, so that they did not bear grain. Still other seed fell on good soil. It came up, grew and produced a crop, multiplying thirty, sixty, or even a hundred times." Then Jesus said, "He who has ears to hear, let him hear." When He was alone, the Twelve and the others around Him asked Him about the parables. He told them, "The secret of the kingdom of God has been given to you. But to those on the outside everything is said in parables so that, "they may be ever seeing but never perceiving, and ever hearing but never understanding; otherwise they might turn and be forgiven!"* (Mark 4:1-12 NIV)

This is a huge benefit to serving and submitting to your leader. There is greater growth potential in being a follower than in being a part of the crowd. Step away from the crowd and step into followership to discover the best that the Kingdom of God has to offer.

The Economics of Leadership

Cause and effect, demand and supply, need and solution—these are all components of economics. Leadership has the same economic demands as the gross national product. If there is no demand, there is no need for leadership.

The key to success is to find out what people's problems are and to give the solution. The whole world revolves around the fact that people have needs and someone supplies the need.

Every minister, business owner, executive, governmental office, or leader of any type is in one business. That business is to supply the demand, or in other words, to meet the needs of the needy. The objective is to meet needs, yet each person meets needs differently. In this book, we have been looking at those who do the work, and those who lead and train others to do the work. They have both responsibility and gifts. Need is the common denominator between ministry and leadership. Ministry meets needs, and leadership meets needs. Ministry demands grace, mercy, and power to meet people's felt needs. Leadership raises up followers to meet people's felt needs. Leadership demands coaching accountability and execution to build the people to meet the felt needs of others. *Needership* is needed for *followership*, and *followership* is needed for *leadership*. Jesus first created a ministry culture and then established a leadership culture in His organization.

We see this in Matthew 9:35-38:

> *Then Jesus went about all the cities and villages, teaching in their synagogues, preaching the gospel of the kingdom,*

and healing every sickness and every disease among the people. But when He saw the multitudes, He was moved with compassion for them, because they were weary and scattered, like sheep having no shepherd. Then He said to His disciples, "The harvest truly is plentiful, but the laborers are few. Therefore pray the Lord of the harvest to send out laborers into His harvest."

Jesus was busy doing the ministry Himself and noticed that all of His ministry work didn't have a major impact on the needs of the people; they were still troubled and helpless. What was the solution to this problem? Obviously it was not enough for the greatest minister of all time to minister to them; they needed more. They needed people to be trained to lead them, not simply minister to them. They were sheep without leaders. Jesus then started training those who were with Him to think differently. He said, *"The harvest is large, but the workers are few."* Or in modern terms: the needs are great, so we must raise people up who will meet those needs. Let's stop thinking like ministers; let's think as leaders. Let your prayers be for more leaders with ministry in their heart. The five-fold ministry is not to do the work of the ministry but to train those who are to do the work of the ministry.

A ministry or church that first develops a strong leadership culture must also eventually develop an equally strong ministry culture, and vice versa. But once there are strong leadership and ministry cultures, your ministry will be a force to be reckoned with.

Ministry and Leadership in Partnership

In the Book of Acts chapter 6 we see something similar regarding strong leadership and ministry cultures working within the same organization:

At that time, as the number of disciples grew, Greek-speaking Jews complained about the Hebrew-speaking Jews. The Greek-speaking Jews claimed that the widows among them were neglected every day when food and other assistance was distributed. The twelve apostles called all the disciples together and told them, "It's not right for us to give up God's word in order to distribute food. So, brothers and sisters, choose seven men whom the people know are spiritually wise. We will put them in charge of this problem. However, we will devote ourselves to praying and to serving in ways that are related to the word." The suggestion pleased the whole group. So they chose Stephen, who was a man full of faith and the Holy Spirit, and they chose Philip, Prochorus, Nicanor, Timon, Parmenas, and Nicolaus, who had converted to Judaism in the city of Antioch. The disciples had these men stand in front of the apostles, who prayed and placed their hands on these seven men. The word of God continued to spread, and the number of disciples in Jerusalem grew very large. A large number of priests accepted the faith (Acts 6:1-7 GWD).

The first thing that we should take note of is that the number of disciples was growing—from the twelve to what the King James version calls "a multitude" of disciples. The Lord of the Harvest was answering the prayers of the disciples. There is not one ministry in operation that couldn't benefit from a multitude of disciples. I'm not talking about a multitude of people who need ministry, but a multitude of people who are students of the Word of God and ready for ministry. In Acts, there were a multitude of leaders who were waiting for their opportunity to meet the needs of the harvest. In addition there were complaints. These types of "complaints" revealed needs that called for leaders to meet them. The complaints would have been a problem if Jesus and His disciples had not developed a strong leadership and ministry culture. Leaders with a ministry understanding were ready to meet the need. We should never be totally caught off guard when a need arises. We will have the provision ready when the need arises if we have been focusing on leadership, followership, and needership. We need people on our team who are always looking to meet needs and who possess intellectual curiosity.

Did you notice how the chief leaders responded to the need? They didn't stop doing what they had been mandated to do in order to meet the pressing needs. This is not because the need was not urgent. It was an urgent need for the *disciples* to meet, not the chief leaders. The disciples had such a strong leadership culture that the chief leader didn't even pick the disciples who would solve the problem. The followers picked those from among themselves to work. A culture with followers who have a strong leadership dynamic and a strong ministry focus will develop mature followers who can be trusted and not micro-managed.

Because we have been cultivating this culture in our organization, we find that more and more of our leaders are developing followers by focusing on building teams. We have a gentleman in our church who felt prompted to start a prison outreach. Once he got everything in place, he began to cultivate a team around the vision. Each person on the team found a place for his or her gifts and talents to function. I loved watching this process because it is a ministry of our church, but I didn't have to do anything other than give my permission. The gentleman brought me his dream, I told him to go to our ministry development department, which helped him work through any gaps in the vision, structure, and administrative process. Then he started the recruiting process and he formed and trained a team. It was smooth, as far as I know. Not once did I have to be engaged with the details. If you have this kind of culture in your organization, it will release you to focus on the macro-management instead of the micro-management. This will allow you to simply pray for them, place your hand on them, and commission them to the work.

We must understand that we cannot be only needership oriented, because this could cause us to be so mercy driven that we would leave the mandate to meet the pressing crisis. This would be devastating to the organization in the long haul if not corrected and brought back into balance.

I don't want to finish this thought without giving some instruction to followers about needership. This type of culture operates under five dynamics: first, see the need; second, think on the need; third, meet the need; fourth, see that the need is continually met through a focus-team; and fifth, make everyone feel that they are needed and a part of the team that meets needs. I see this process in how our prison outreach has come to pass. But this is happening all the time. We have released people to become innovators and not just task people. One couple developed a meeting called Meet the Pastors, for anyone who is interested in becoming a part of the vision or who wants to know more about the organization. We also have a monthly church outreach that is envisioned, directed, and sustained by a different department each month. This was my wife's brilliant idea. She wanted an outreach that empowered the church to come up with new and innovative ideas every month. It is working and we are now reaching demographics we usually would not. The goal is to empower people to become a vital part of the organization.

In the book *The Disney Way,* authors Bill Capodagali and Lynn Jackson give us insights on one of the greatest and most creative organizations in the earth and how they empower their team:

> When Walt Disney was at the helm of the company, everyone was invited to voice their opinions and to make suggestions—in fact, not just invited but required. The corporate hierarchy dissolved when it came to offering ideas for improving a movie script, a theme park ride, or an animated sequence. Anyone could bring suggestions for

cartoons and features to Walt himself. Basically, the same holds true today, but the size of the company makes a casual approach impractical. The company does provide regular opportunities to harvest good ideas from all corners of the organizations, however. In a thrice-yearly event known as the Gong Show, named after a television program popular in the 1970s and '80s, animators, secretaries, and anyone else who thinks he or she has a good idea can formally make a pitch to a panel of top brass that includes CEO Michael Eisner, vice chairman of the board Roy Disney, executive vice president of animation Tom Schumacher, and president of the animation division Peter Schneider. *Hercules*, for example, grew from an animator's idea that a man is judged by his inner strength and not his outer strength.

The Disney Way authors also make it very clear that a culture such as this is a powerful learning experience for the employees to understand what and why one idea works and another doesn't work. The authors write,

> It is a tough milieu because the listeners at the table provide immediate and honest reactions. "You must have immediate communication and not worry about peoples ego's and feelings," Schneider says. "If you do that enough and people do not get fired or demoted, they begin to understand that no matter how good, bad, or indifferent the idea, it can be expressed, accepted, and considered."

Some followers want leadership because they feel that only leaders get heard. In a followership culture we must develop a way for followers to think like leaders and feel free to share their hopes, dreams, ideas, and suggestions. I believe that if we give people a safe harbor to express their brilliance, they will shine.

Followership and Efficacy

The way a person follows the leader determines the organization's effectiveness. Effectiveness means, "something brought about by a cause or agent; a result."[2] Followers should have confidence in their ability to bring about and sustain change. This is called "efficacy" which is "the power to produce an effect."[3] The profile of your organization, whether ministry or business, should be based upon a problem that you are solving or a need that you are fulfilling. What is your organization's efficacy? What is your efficacy as a leader or as a follower? No matter what your position is, you must be effective in meeting needs and solving problems; otherwise, you will end up being obsolete as an organization, leader, and/or follower.

Efficacy is something that must be challenged. Leaders, you must be able to challenge those who follow in their ability to effect any situation. Next levels are reached through an increase in efficacy. Followers, you must allow your leaders to challenge your level of effectiveness. If you cannot see yourself fixing a problem or overcoming an obstacle, and if you cannot envision yourself becoming the best at whatever is set before you, you possess a low level of efficacy. Leaders need people on the team who believe that they can achieve, accomplish, and bring about a desired effect at any cost. The number one sign of a low efficacy level is an excuse. Excuses tie your leader's hands, keeping them from the ability to coach you into another level. There is no other option for your leader but to replace you.

Endnotes

1. McClintock and Strong's Cyclopedia of Biblical, Theological and Ecclesiastical Literature. Copyright © 2000, 2003 by Biblesoft, Inc. All rights reserved.

2. *Merriam-Webster's Collegiate Dictionary,* 11th ed. s.v., "Effectiveness."

3. *Merriam-Webster's Collegiate Dictionary,* 11th ed. s.v., "Efficacy."

CHAPTER SIXTEEN

OBEY THE LAWS

A FEW LAWS MUST be obeyed in order to have uncommon success. Law is the legislative pronouncement of rules to guide one's actions in society; a standard; or a principle of behavior. Respect and obedience to universal laws will yield long-lasting results in life, business, and ministry. The following are a few laws that will help you in serving your leader with excellence and produce outstanding personal results.

The Law of Agreement

The law of agreement aligns one person's power, faith, and abilities with another person's in order to reach a common goal. We can only agree upon things which involve similarity of belief. I know that some choose "to agree to disagree" in order to stop or prevent an argument, but after agreeing to disagree, there is still no more unity or opportunity for advancement involved. If there is a difference of beliefs, then agreement cannot be developed. Unity is a by-product of agreement. This makes it clear that we cannot walk together unless we agree. It is funny to see people trying to align and unify without actual agreement. Looking at Amos 3:3, we all know the answer is no! *"Can two walk together, unless they are agreed?"* We can never walk together without agreement. So the law of agreement works when you first reinforce your belief systems and then align with others with the same belief systems to create a synergy that will produce unimaginable power and multiplication. Magnify what you can achieve by joining with someone who also possesses talents.

If we pay attention we will see that the market place is formulated with powerful alliances such as Taco Bell and Pizza Hut partnerships. If you haven't noticed, Pizza Hut restaurants are passing away and their new direction has become partnering with the drive-thru relationships that are available to them. I know this only because of an opportunity that was granted to me to do some corporate coaching with an organization which owned many Pizza Hut restaurants. We also see the power of agreement with Apple and AT&T with the iPhone phenomenon, and KLM and Delta Airlines. Another powerful agreement has been the Embassy Suites with Build-a-Bear Workshops, which showed huge financial numbers of profitability for both organizations. Build-a-Bear offers the customers of Embassy Suites an overnight pack for their family teddy bears.

> Kids will have fun pampering their stuffed animal friends with the Build-A-Bear Workshop Sleep Over pack that includes a bear-sized Embassy Suites terry robe or Embassy Suites draw-string pajama pants and t-shirt just right for bears who want to relax and unwind; cozy Embassy Suites slippers; a shower kit with shower cap, plush soap and lotion to keep furry friends feeling fresh and clean; and a $5 Bear Buck$® gift card to use at Build-A-Bear Workshop, all in a cool carryall.[1]

Each of these powerful alliances has found the law of agreement to maximize their customer base and productivity.

The law of agreement moves God as it creates unity. Matthew 18:19-20 shows us that God answers the prayers of agreement.

> *Again I say to you that if two of you agree on earth concerning anything that they ask, it will be done for them by My Father in heaven. For where two or three are gathered together in My name, I am there in the midst of them.*

God not only wants to answer the prayers of those who agree together on earth, but God actually wants to spend time and fellowship with people who believe in something enough that they would align together to get it done. Knowledge of the Law of Agreement will cause you to surround yourself with people who have the same belief systems and the same principles. All of our belief systems and principles should be biblically based; this is the only way common ground is found. Agree to live the best life available by living in agreement with God and those who do the same.

Law of Association

We have already spent a lot of time on association, but in this section I would like to encourage balanced association. We should have three groups of associations in our lives. First are those whom you are counseling, discipling, or winning to the Lord. Second are those whom you fellowship with, which is the company that you keep and the peers whom you influence and are influenced by. Surround yourself with peers who pressure you into being a great parent, a great spouse, a great worker, a great minister, or a great follower and leader-servant. Third, you must have someone whom you look up to; in order to be healthy and challenged, you must have mentors—those whom you serve and are submitted to.

I personally have those whom I am mentoring in business and ministry as a coach and spiritual father. I also have many friends and peers that I talk to on a weekly and monthly basis, which benefits both of us. I also have a strong group of leaders in my life. I was saved in November 1988, and I have had the same leadership voices speaking into my life ever since then. I maintain these long-term mentoring relationships by maintaining a teachable spirit and a lifestyle of learning. Of course I have added many other mentors personally, and through books, CDs, and DVDs.

A balance of association will cause you to maintain a healthy view and healthy communication. You communicate with each level differently. Posture yourself to teach and train those whom you disciple and mentor. Fellowship, align, and influence your peers to good works.

One major rule that will keep you from a lot of trouble is that you should never, ever counsel down. Don't go to your disciples with problems that you have personally, ministerially, or otherwise. Never talk to them about how frustrated you feel with your position or your leader. Never talk to anybody about something that they have no power to change. These relationships are not in place for you to get counsel but for you to give counsel. You can counsel across or up, but avoid sharing intimate details and your problems with your spiritual children just as you would not share all of your problems with your natural children. Keep these associations innocent, and they will serve you as you serve them. Talk to your peers about personal problems and develop covenants of accountability if it is necessary. Take major issues to your leaders and allow them to instruct you and coach you to your maximum potential.

I cry on the shoulders of my peers and I get instruction from my mentors. When I am with my mentors I want to receive instruction and wisdom. I can also receive this from my peers, but I will look for a little more comfort from my peers. Not because I don't want my mentors to know my problems, but I don't want to make that relationship a relationship of comfort but keep it one of coaching. I talk to them about areas in which I need improvement, help, and change.

Law of Attraction

Develop the ability to attract others to the work. You must have something within you that will attract people to you, as mentioned earlier. You also must have something within so that you will be attractive for a leader to want to involve you in their vision. Attraction works both ways.

According to John Maxwell in his book *Developing the Leader Within You,* you must develop as a leader. If you are a level four leader, you will not be able to attract and keep level eight leaders. Your strength of leadership will always attract a lesser strength of leader to yourself and your organization. A level four leader will only be able to attract a level three or below leader.

You must grow as a leader yourself if you want to attract better workers and leaders. You must be willing to grow as a leader in order to be recruited by a level nine or ten leader. The better leader you are, the more attractive you will be. The kind of servant you are will determine the kind of leader you will be. Your leadership abilities and skills will determine your attractiveness to others.

Law of Excellence

Excellence means to throw farther than anyone else on a consistent basis. To throw farther once is not excellence; it must be something that can be reproduced on demand. Excellence is systematic and processed. McDonalds is not excellent because they serve the best burgers around; their excellence is found in their system, which enables them to produce the same results nearly perfectly each time. Not only is their business model systems-based, but each burger is so systematic that they have virtually fool-proofed it; anyone can be easily trained to make the burgers. This means that they have paid great attention to details. People of excellence are systematic and pay close attention to details.

In our organization, we always look to systemize and process every new and creative idea. If we can't build a system around it, than we treat it as an isolated event. Like I mentioned in the previous chapter, we use a system that we call a pipeline to develop leaders. We also use a system for guest relations. We have a detailed system for follow-up and assimilation. We build a system for everything so that we can maintain the details as we continue to develop the larger picture.

Paying close attention to details is the key to living above the norm.

> *For which of you, intending to build a tower, does not sit down first and count the cost, whether he has enough to finish it — lest, after he has laid the foundation, and is not able to finish, all who see it begin to mock him, saying, "This man began to build and was not able to finish." Or what king, going to make war against another king, does not sit down first and consider whether he is able with ten thousand to meet him who comes against him with twenty thousand? Or else, while the other is still a great way off, he sends a delegation and asks conditions of peace. So likewise, whoever of you does not forsake all that he has cannot be My disciple"* (Luke 14:28-33).

Operate in excellence by building a detailed system for every area of your life. Systems will help you produce the desired results on a consistent basis. One thing that I always remember is to build on my strengths passionately and manage my weaknesses through systems. I am a visionary. All visionaries can lose sight of what is necessary today. So I have people on my team who help me see what is current so that I don't walk over people in order to get to the future that I see.

Another thing that we use as a part of our system is a D.I.S.C. personality profile test to help us put people in the right place on the team. We want to make sure that the people who are on the team are in a place where they can thrive and benefit the organization and where they can enjoy good results. Of course, we don't completely rely on these tools, but we won't move without these tools, just in case we miss something. The science of the D.I.S.C. profile is intricate, and I suggest that you get someone who understands how to implement the test to do so. We have a person on our team who has studied how to give and to interpret these tests in our organization.

The Law of Faithfulness

As a leader, the hardest to deal with is an unfaithful servant. The writer of Proverbs in 25:19 says, *"Putting confidence in an unreliable person in times of trouble is like chewing with a toothache or walking on a lame foot"* (NLT). I have learned the truth of this statement from experience. It seems that it is easiest to be unreliable at the most sensitive times. Faithfulness is based upon a decision to commit to a vision and to see the vision fulfilled with excellence during hard times. Part of making a commitment is saying yes to the right things and keeping your word no matter what. The Bible says in James 5:12,

> *Above all, my brothers, do not swear—not by heaven or by earth or by anything else. Let your 'Yes' be yes, and your 'No' no, or you will be condemned* (NIV).

"Above all" is a giant statement. I believe that this statement identifies God's heart toward keeping your word. Above all, keep your word. Above all, don't be lukewarm. Either be committed or be unreliable; you can't be both, so choose.

The last thing a leader needs is excuses. If you are asked by your leader to do something, he or she should never have to come back to you to find out why it wasn't done. Partial fulfillment or complete failure to accomplish what you were asked to do will result in a breakdown of your leader's trust and confidence in you. If you failed, then be repentant; let your leader know that you know you failed them and that your priority is to never let that happen again.

Listen to this Scripture, Proverbs 25:19: *"Confidence in an unfaithful man in time of trouble is like a bad tooth and a foot out of joint."*

There are few things worse to a leader than a servant-leader who fails to come through or is slow to do so. Make up your mind that God and your leader will never need to repeat themselves again. They will feel confident to give you more responsibility as you prove yourself trustworthy. I have people on my team whom I can talk to once and they get the job done. I never have to check on whether or not they have finished the work. I see it operating in the organization. I also have some who are faithful and loyal but they are developing confidence, and it is OK for them to make a mistake. I would rather have a finished product that needs a little tweaking than to have someone who doesn't finish because they don't have confidence to make a mistake.

I also have people on my team that I have to check on over and over to see whether or not they have finished the work. If these people don't start showing progress very quickly, their life expectancy on the team is growing shorter quickly. I may love all these people, but we can never allow our feelings to hold us back from doing what is right for the organization. If I don't give these people a way out, they will end up frustrating me, and I will end up frustrating them. Every time I have to check whether or not a person has finished a project, I have to do their job. Now, there is a season of training and development, but some who know what they are doing simply don't do it. If I have to keep reiterating myself over and over regarding the same thing, that person is pulling me out of my focus and directives in order to do their job. Conversely, I will be forced to quickly look for another person if they prove themselves slow to move or neglectful to do what was asked.

Faithfully steward what God has entrusted you with, and be prepared for more opportunities to come your way. The next Scripture is a picture of what increased opportunity looks like:

> *His master replied, "Well done, good and faithful servant! You have been faithful with a few things; I will put you in charge of many things. Come and share your master's happiness!" The man with the two talents also came. "Master," he said, "you entrusted me with two talents; see, I have gained two more." His master replied, "Well done, good and faithful servant! You have been faithful with a few things; I will put you in charge of many things. Come and share your master's happiness!" Then the man who had received the one talent came. "Master," he said, "I knew that you are a hard man, harvesting where you have not sown and gathering where you have not scattered seed. So I was afraid and went out and hid your talent in the ground. See, here is what belongs to you." His master replied, "You wicked, lazy servant! So you knew that I harvest where I have not sown and gather where I have not scattered seed? Well then, you should have put my money on deposit with the bankers, so that when I returned I would have received it back with interest. Take the talent from him and give it to the one who has the ten talents. For everyone who has will be given more, and he will have an abundance. Whoever does not have, even what he has will be taken from him. And throw that worthless servant outside, into the darkness, where there will be weeping and gnashing of teeth"* (Matthew 25:21-30 NIV).

The law of faithfulness will introduce you to the law of increase. God is looking to and fro to see who is faithful in the earth and to see where He can release His blessing and increase.

Plasticity vs. Elasticity

Recently I traveled to California to help a pastor friend go to the next level. Before I got there, I challenged them to reach higher and to press deeper through prayer and in faith, believing God to move on their behalf. The results were dynamic. We had a very effective time. A short time later, we went back with hopes of taking another level. I preached, taught, and ministered with all of my heart. God in His mercy helped people, but the ministry and organization didn't seem to possess a new level or even maintain the previous level.

As I was riding back to the airport, God spoke to me the word *plasticity.* Plasticity means "the property of a solid body whereby it undergoes a permanent change in shape or size when subjected to a stress exceeding a particular value, called the yield value."[2] What God was telling me is that through the first trip, the church and its leadership was stretched and expanded to another level—not only during the meetings, but also in preparation for the meetings. They pressed hard with prayer and faith, yet after the meeting, they went back to what was normal for them, instead of maintaining the new level by abandoning the old pattern and continuing to do what it took to get to that new level. They stretched and reached out and then returned back to the previous form, where it was comfortable. Elasticity means "the property of returning to an initial form."[3] This leader and his team should have kept the press, which caused gain. Instead, they were elastic.

Make sure that you have plasticity instead of elasticity. People think that in order to get good results, they should only exert temporary good effort. This theory could not be further from the truth. The truth is that in order to get good results, you must exert excellent effort; and in order to achieve excellent results, you must exert outstanding effort; and in order to gain outstanding results, you must exert unnatural effort. Whatever effort you exert to get to a certain position, you must continue that energy and more in order to keep it. On top of that, if you desire to go another level from your current position, you will have to add to the current efforts another level of great effort—but you can work smarter to multiply the efforts instead of simply adding to the efforts.

Elasticity is backsliding, and plasticity is transforming into the next level. Romans 12:2 says that we are transformed through the renewing of our minds. Plasticity is a mind-set, not a position. The position follows the mind-set. Move there and maintain it in your mind; your effort will follow, and then your position will follow. The key focus is to "maintain it."

Endnotes

1. Hilton World-Wide press release, http://phx.corporate-ir.net/phoenix. zhtml?c=88577&p=irol-newsArticleOther_pf&ID=1009938.

2. *Merriam-Webster's Collegiate Dictionary,* 11th ed., s.v., "Plasticity."

3. *Merriam-Webster's Collegiate Dictionary,* 11th ed., s.v., "Elasticity."

CHAPTER SEVENTEEN

OIL FLOWS DOWN

IN THIS CHAPTER WE will discuss the benefits of unity, the anointing, and the commanded blessing that are available to followers for their service of love.

> *For God is not unjust to forget your work and labor of love which you have shown toward His name, in that you have ministered to the saints, and do minister* (Hebrews 6:10-11).

God keeps an account of all of the work and service that you perform in the Kingdom of God. God will never allow the work that you do to be wasted; He will make sure that you will profit from the work that you perform. I have served many people, and I believe I am receiving benefits from all of the service that I performed. I can testify that the greater my submission to authority, the greater the favor that was released into my life. Whenever one of the men or women whom I have served experience a new breakthrough or dimension to their lives or ministry, I rejoice because I believe that I will experience the same favor in my future because of the time I spent serving their vision.

In Psalm 133, we see unity, anointing, and a command to be blessed. Let's read:

> *Behold, how good and how pleasant it is for brethren to dwell together in unity! It is like the precious oil upon the head, running down on the beard, the beard of Aaron, running down on the edge of his garments. It is like the dew of Hermon, descending upon the mountains of Zion; for there the Lord commanded the blessing—life forevermore.*

If we know that unity is good and pleasant, then disunity must be bad and ugly. The Law of Agreement comes into play with unity. Unity is only built upon individuals agreeing on one or more beliefs. It is like the symbol of holy separation unto purpose, flowing perfectly to cover the whole body. It is like the dew of Hermon descending: unity doesn't start from the bottom; unity starts at the top.

Unity starts with joining a leader who has a full-bodied vision, with leaders who have a Kingdom vision. If the leader doesn't have a Kingdom vision, then the followers won't have a full-bodied vision and Kingdom vision. Unity must be established through a purpose-driven vision to establish God's Kingdom. If the vision for a church doesn't include God's Kingdom, God won't allow it to stand. Genesis 11:5-7 says,

> *But the Lord came down to see the city and the tower that the men were building. The Lord said, "If as one people speaking the same language they have begun to do this, then nothing they plan to do will be impossible for them. Come, let us go down and confuse their language so they will not understand each other* (NIV).

The devil learned something from this experience, and he has been using this strategy ever since. He realized then that if unity could accomplish anything, then disunity could prevent all things. Jesus said it this way, a *"house divided against itself will not stand"* (Matt. 12:25). For the sake of growth and increase, your leader needs for you to fight for unity, rather than agreeing to disagree! The greatest momentum-stealer is disunity. Disunity will stop all growth and increase in its tracks. If you allow the devil to use you to bring or perpetuate disunity, you will be responsible for the inevitable breakdown of God's work.

There is a different strategy for leading a volunteer base team verses a fulltime paid team. But one thing is for sure; everybody on either team must be a team player in order for any organization to thrive. In the corporate world, interoffice disunity is dangerous to the culture of the organization. In a corporate setting, a lack of unity may break down the morale enough for people to jump ship and look for a position elsewhere. In a church organization there could be even greater disasters at hand. Look at this statistic:

> Eighty-five percent of pastors said their greatest problem is they are sick and tired of dealing with problem people, such as disgruntled elders, deacons, worship leaders, worship teams, board members, and associate pastors. Ninety percent said the hardest thing about ministry is dealing with uncooperative people.[1]

No matter what environment you work in, there must be an everyday fight for unity.

The key to keeping unity around a purpose-driven vision is communication. The tower of Babel ceased when God confused the language of the builders. On the day of Pentecost, God restored the ability to communicate so that building would never be hindered through the lack of communication. The Holy Spirit delivered to mankind the gift of communication. Simply asking the Holy Spirit to help you understand the vision of the leader will help you to fully connect, and will give you the determination to protect that vision at all costs.

Often people leave an organization because it is missing something that they think should be in place. They choose to move on instead of joining the vision and filling that gap. If every person just leaves, then the gaps will never be filled. The gaps of every organization should be filled with someone who has passion, even if that passion is founded in frustration.

Unity in the Bigger Picture

So many people abort their opportunities because they can't see beyond their personal issues to the bigger picture. They have developed a blind spot or, as psychologists call it, a "scotoma." They have been blinded so they cannot see that they are the answer to the problem and the key to producing a breakthrough. Daniel shows the power of unity and how it affects heaven and earth. Daniel 10:7-9 says,

> *And I, Daniel, alone saw the vision, for the men who were with me did not see the vision; but a great terror fell upon them, so that they fled to hide themselves. Therefore I was left alone when I saw this great vision, and no strength remained in me; for my vigor was turned to frailty in me, and I retained no strength. Yet I heard the sound of his words; and while I heard the sound of his words I was in a deep sleep on my face, with my face to the ground.*

Daniel was left alone because those with him didn't see the vision. They didn't understand what was going on, so they ran away. In Daniel 10:12-14, we see,

> *Then he said to me, "Do not fear, Daniel, for from the first day that you set your heart to understand, and to humble yourself before your God, your words were heard; and I have come because of your words. But the prince of the kingdom of*

> *Persia withstood me twenty-one days; and behold, Michael,*
> *one of the chief princes, came to help me, for I had been left*
> *alone there with the kings of Persia. Now I have come to make*
> *you understand what will happen to your people in the latter*
> *days, for the vision refers to many days yet to come."*

Here we see that the angel of the Lord finally showed up after fighting in the heavens for 21 days. Then in verse 13, the angel says, *"for I had been left alone there with the kings of Persia."* Now we see that the angel of the Lord was left alone to fight on his own. Understand that every believer has angels assigned to them and that these angels are engaged in the heavens as we are engaged on earth. When we join together on earth, our assigned angels join together in the heavens in order to bring to pass whatever is being asked for on earth. Sometimes we make decisions without thinking about how it will affect eternity and the Kingdom of God. If we could maintain an eternal perspective, we would find more opportunities for unity. What we do in the seen world affects the unseen more than we know. How many building projects or church plants or humanitarian works have been aborted or delayed because people have stepped away from the vision? What we do here matters in eternity, so keep an eternal perspective and benefit the Kingdom of God by fighting for true unity.

Both leaders and followers have to make tough decisions all the time. Many times these tough choices will force others to make choices themselves. The misconception is that unity brings everyone together when the truth is exactly the opposite. Unity actually separates. When my wife and I needed to make some tough decisions in the direction of our church, some of the people on our team made the decision to talk about how they didn't agree with our decisions, while all along separating themselves from the vision that we were casting. They began to gossip and complain to others. After awhile you could see the separation in their heart by their posture and actions. The ones who used to come early and stay late started missing meetings. The ones that used to support financially began to withhold their gifts. Those who used to sit near to us began to sit in the back. Those who used to laugh at our jokes stopped laughing and started frowning. The ones who said, "We are with you forever no matter what!" disappeared. When these signs start to show, put it on your calendar that they will be leaving soon if they can't see past their disapproval and align again with the eternal vision. At the same time we saw some of these who were very close friends with the disgruntled followers separate to the vision. As they separated to the vision they also separated from those friends; not by our request nor by their desire, but because unity brings division. The people who had a problem with me had a problem with those on the team that would support us. They held unto their personal differences and opinions and refused the Kingdom vision. Here we are years later, the past being 20/20 vision, and we can see that those who couldn't keep an eternal perspective are no better off and we are progressing in the eternal vision.

Sometimes followers don't realize that a leader also may disagree with the decision that they are making, yet the leader must obey the leading of the Lord and do what is necessary for the benefit of the organization. Many things that my wife and I wanted to do regarding the cause and mandate of the organizations we led and lead we couldn't do because it wouldn't promote God's culture nor benefit the organization. You can never fight for unity and yourself at the same time. One has to give. Unity calls for you to take the humble road, to let go of your rights and hurt feelings, to relinquish being right. The Bible tells us that strife can only come from being carnal.

> *For ye are yet carnal: for whereas there is among you envying, and strife, and divisions, are ye not carnal, and walk as men?* (1 Corinthians 3:3 KJV)

Unity flows like the oil from Aaron's beard and descends like the dew on the mountains. Unity allows you to join with the vision, anointing, and favor of the leader whom you serve. Remember, unity cannot flow upwards;

unity must flow downwards. A leader cannot join the vision of the servant just as *"the disciple is not above his master"* (Luke 6:40 KJV). The power of belonging to something greater than yourself is that you can benefit from being a part of something significant, something you could never produce by yourself. Every person needs to feel significant. We all need to feel as if we are a part of something bigger than ourselves. We must never forget that when we serve someone else's vision they may very well end up becoming a gatekeeper for us in the future.

I have walked through several major doors which were open to me because I served men of God without asking for anything from them. I served and God moved upon them to open the doors without me manipulating or striving for these doors to open. For years I have served Pastor Phil Munsey, and a few years ago he interviewed me on TBN before a television audience of millions of viewers. After that he introduced me to Dr. Oral Roberts, opening for me to have a private audience with Dr. Oral where he prayed for me and imparted to me the anointing to believe God. I could continue to list one event after another of how God has caused my seeds of service to grow and flourish into wonderful open doors. Serve your way to the top.

God-Fearing Unity

God commands a blessing when God-fearing unity is present. God-fearing unity is birthed from a Kingdom-building and purpose-driven vision. The builders of the tower of Babel had a unified vision, but God could not bless it because it didn't have God's name on it. A few years ago in California, a gang of bank robbers went into a bank with the common vision of robbing the bank. When they walked out of the bank, justice was waiting for them, and they began fighting for survival. One by one they were stopped. Justice will overcome any plot which was birthed from evil intentions, unified or not.

The blessing of the Lord will only be upon unified efforts for a common goal to build and benefit the Kingdom of God. You may be reading this book as a businessperson and wonder how your business builds the Kingdom of God. God is as eager for you to build your business as He is for a church or a ministry to be built, as long as you include God in your business affairs. You see your business as a ministry, and you see increase in your life as an opportunity to be a giver and a blessing—first to the house of God and secondly to others.

I have heard many people talk about kings and priests joining together to build the Kingdom of God: the king being a business person who can exchange a financial gift for the anointing and blessing of the priest; the priest being the one who receives the gift and transfers a blessing and anointing to the king to go and increase more and more. I am not sure of the terms *kings* and *priests,* but I am sure of the principle that there must be unity amongst those who work in the ministry and those who work in the marketplace. I see this principle with Melchizedek and Abram in Genesis 14 after Abram went to war and won:

> And the king of Sodom went out to meet him at the Valley of Shaveh (that is, the King's Valley), after his return from the defeat of Chedorlaomer and the kings who were with him. Then Melchizedek king of Salem brought out bread and wine; he was the priest of God Most High. And he blessed him and said: "Blessed be Abram of God Most High, Possessor of heaven and earth; and blessed be God Most High, Who has delivered your enemies into your hand." And he gave him a tithe of all. Now the king of Sodom said to Abram, "Give me the persons, and take the goods for yourself." But Abram said to the king of Sodom, "I have raised my hand to the Lord, God Most High, the Possessor of heaven and earth, that I will take nothing, from a thread to a sandal strap, and that I will not take anything that is yours, lest

you should say, 'I have made Abram rich'—except only what the young men have eaten, and the portion of the men who went with me: Aner, Eshcol, and Mamre; let them take their portion" (Genesis 14:17-24).

Abraham had the opportunity to align himself with the King of Sodom, and he could have been rich, but instead he chose to shake hands with God through His priest and get rich from the hand of God. The blessing of God was released on Abram through the priest of God after the gift or tithe was brought to the priest. Abram was not a king, but Melchizedek was a priest. The principle still stands that your business must have a greater purpose than mere existence. Your business must exist for the building of the Kingdom of God. Every time you bring the tithe to the house of God, a blessing for you to go out and increase comes upon you.

My good friend Joel Luce has increased yearly from this principle. Joel believes so strongly in giving that he and his wife say that they have a need to give. He has no problem giving to the work of the Kingdom, so God has no problem prospering him. Joel increased every year until he actually was able to buy the company that he worked for, a $50,000,000 company; he increased from working for the company to becoming the CEO and owner of the company. This kind of progress can come upon each of us if we put the Kingdom first.

There was a time that we were dealing with a financial lull in the church. I felt prompted to check the giving of our leaders to see how they were doing. Shocked by the results, it didn't take long for me to realize what was taking place. If those who follow the vision can't get behind the vision by word, deed and financially, then they will not be able to rightly encourage people to lay down their lives for the cause. Once we made the necessary changes, the lull lifted.

It is important that everyone in the organization participates as givers, especially if the organization is a church or non-profit. Find unity with the work of the Kingdom, and make sure that you have unity in your business. Then you will see the increase of God move upon you and your business. Unity is the only growth mechanism; we can never grow beyond our present level of unity. If you desire for your church to grow, if you desire your business to grow, if you desire for your family to grow deeper in love, grow the unity within these areas. If they are not growing, then look at the level of unity and increase it in every way.

> *Behold, how good and how pleasant it is for brethren to dwell together in unity! It is like the precious ointment upon the head, running down on the beard, the beard of Aaron, running down on the edge of his garments. It is like the dew of Hermon, descending upon the mountains of Zion; for there the Lord commanded the blessing—life forevermore* (Psalm 133).

In this Scripture you can see the plan of God for the release of His blessing. The foundation of the commanded blessing is unity; God blesses unity. God actually commands the blessing when He finds unity. The word *command* comes from the word *tsavah* (tsaw-vaw'), which means "to constitute or enjoin."[2] God wants to enjoin Himself to whatever we are doing in unity for His name's sake. God doesn't enjoin Himself to things that are going to fail. Unity is the secret to not failing. God sent His disciples out two by two so that they could pick one another up if need be and keep each other accountable. *We* are to keep each other from failing by promoting unity. God will enjoin Himself to us and guarantee the *brakah* (ber-aw-kaw'), which means benediction; by implication prosperity: blessing, liberal, pool, present.[3] Join the ranks of unity, and God will bring the blessing.

The Anointing

The anointing of your leader is available for you through association, to operate in for your own personal life and ministry. Not only do you reap where you have sown, but you also reap what you have sown into. Let's look at Matthew 10:

> *He who finds his life shall lose it. And he who loses his life for My sake shall find it. He who receives you receives Me, and he who receives Me receives Him who sent Me. He who receives a prophet in the name of a prophet shall receive a prophet's reward. And he who receives a just one in the name of a just one will receive a just one's reward. And whoever shall give to one of these little ones a cup of cold water to drink, only in the name of a disciple, truly I say to you, He shall in no way lose his reward* (Matthew 10: 39-42 MKJV).

You and I deserve to be rewarded with the lift and anointing that rests on the leaders with whom we serve and associate. First Samuel 10:9 reads,

> *And it happened when he had turned his back to go from Samuel, God changed him with another heart. And all those signs came on that day. And they came there to the hill, behold, a company of prophets met him. And the Spirit of God came on him, and he prophesied among them. And it happened when all who knew him before saw him, behold, he prophesied among the prophets. And the people said to one another, What is this that has happened to the son of Kish? Is Saul also among the prophets? And a man from there answered and said, And who is their father? Therefore it became a proverb, Is Saul also among the prophets?* (1 Samuel 10:9-12 MKJV)

Even in the Old Testament, we see this principle in operation when the prophet Elisha sent his servant with the prophet's staff in hand to raise up a dead boy. Second Kings 4:29 tells:

> *Then he said to Gehazi, Bind up your loins and take my staff in your hand, and go. If you meet any man, do not*

greet him. And if any greet you, do not answer him again. And lay my staff on the face of the child. And the mother of the child said, As Jehovah lives, and as your soul lives, I will not leave you. And he arose and followed her. And Gehazi passed on before them and laid the staff on the face of the child... (2 Kings 4:29-31 MKJV).

We can clearly see here that it was practice for the servant to operate with the staff of the prophet. (There were other reasons in this circumstance that the child was not raised up immediately.)

The danger comes in when *presumption* enters the heart of a servant. It takes a long time for a servant to really understand the leader's heart and intentions. *Merriam-Webster's Dictionary* defines presumption in the following ways:

1. The act of presuming, or believing upon probable evidence; the act of assuming or taking for granted; belief upon incomplete proof.

2. Ground for presuming; evidence probable, but not conclusive; strong probability; reasonable supposition; as, the presumption is that an event has taken place.

3. That which is presumed or assumed; that which is supposed or believed to be real or true, on evidence that is probable but not conclusive. "In contradiction to these very plausible presumptions." De Quincey.

4. The act of venturing beyond due bounds; an overstepping of the bounds of reverence, respect, or courtesy;

forward, overconfident, or arrogant opinion or conduct; presumptuousness; arrogance; effrontery.[4]

The fourth definition is by far the most dangerous. When a leader-servant oversteps the boundaries, he or she causes a whole slew of problems with the leader and the team. As a follower, you must operate with a clear understanding of the culture of the leader and the organization. The worst thing that you can ever do is to assume a position or assume a liberty of boundaries that has not been granted to you.

> *Do not put yourself forth in the presence of the king, and do not stand in the place of the great; for it is better that it should be said to you, Come up here, than that you should be put lower in the presence of a noble whom your eyes have seen* (Proverbs 25:6-7 MKJV).

Presumptions will cause you to speak out of turn or to run ahead, but in the wrong direction. The best advice is to try to anticipate the need of the leader and the organization prayerfully; don't choose to set a direction simply because you like it that way. Try to understand how your leaders think and do it their way if possible. Often you will have a better understanding of the needs than your leader, but don't be forward by changing the direction of a project or culture without counsel from them. Bring to them any unforeseen information so that they can make a clear decision and set a directive. If your leader sees that the information is reliable and reasonable they will give your permission to move forward. Presumption will be seen as disobedience in the long run. Your well-meaning intentions will become independence if not handled with care on your side of things. Don't be someone who loves to experiment on the organization—when your leader asks you to accomplish something one way, and you come back with a mess after trying to do it your way. Sometimes you must learn to simply follow orders before you get the freedom to invent new ways. Your leader will recognize your genius in due time. In the meantime, stay in rank and follow orders.

I wrote this book because of what I saw in the following passage—huge presumption:

> *The officer had said to the man of God, "Look, even if the Lord should open the floodgates of the heavens, could this happen?" The man of God had replied, "You will see it with your own eyes, but you will not eat any of it!" And that is exactly what happened to him, for the people trampled him in the gateway, and he died* (2 Kings 7:19-20 NIV).

Don't be a know-it-all! Such people may know a few things, but ultimately they get on everybody's nerves, and their knowledge will be completely rejected, plain and simple. After awhile, I choose to disregard any information that I receive from know-it-alls because they *don't* know it all. It is hard to decipher what they really know, what they are presuming to know, or what they want you to think they know. Also, they often talk too much and out of turn, interrupting conversations and volunteering their opinion when it is not asked for.

> *The words of a wise man's mouth are gracious, but the lips of a fool shall swallow him up; the words of his mouth begin with foolishness, and the end of his talk is raving madness. A fool also multiplies words. No man knows what is to be; who can tell what will be after him?* (Ecclesiastes 10:12-14)

Avoid speaking too much, for your many words will always reveal your foolishness. Be careful of what you say and how you say it, not only in the presence of your leader but also in the presence of your peers and followers. The words that you speak will reveal wisdom or ignorance.

Years ago I preached at a youth retreat for a large church. One evening, God's power manifested in a very specific way. As I prayed for some of the youth, they began to laugh; I mean really laugh. After a while, many of these kids were laughing, and then after a few minutes, some of them started to get out of hand. Not all, but just a handful. One of the girls videotaped it and showed the pastors once they returned home. I was asked to come into the office and talk with the associate and a few other staff members. After I listened to them for about an hour and a half, they came to the conclusion that I needed to apologize for allowing these kids to get out of hand. Well, of course, I couldn't apologize for something that I didn't do or encourage; it simply happened. But the thing that I remember them saying repeatedly was, "I think our pastor would be happy that we are doing this." Over and over, they were trying to correct me in order to please their pastor. I thought to myself, *If you really wanted to please him, you should make a big deal about the girls and boys sneaking out together or about the leader's son who was smoking weed in the bushes late at night.* They thought the news would disturb the pastor, and that rebuking me for allowing something to happen that was truly outside of my control was not as dangerous as the problems that occurred with sex and drugs.

Presumption has false weights and balances. It doesn't see things truthfully. The choices of presumption are foolish and irrational. Ineffective followers who have never been empowered with decision making and the spirit of love and grace make statements like this: "I think that he or she would be happy if we did it this way." Make sure that you really understand your leader's heart before you presume to know their heart; otherwise, you will make a lot of mistakes while guessing all along. Be sure. If you are not sure, then ask and ask and ask until you truly understand how they think.

Presumptuous people don't like taking notes because they think that they will remember or that they already completely understand. Taking notes says to your leader that you respect what they have to say. With this in mind, even if you have heard what they have said a thousand times, you should take notes for respect's sake. Whenever I am with my leaders, I immediately pull out something on which to take notes. I believe it inspires them to tell me things that they have been studying or meditating on. Take notes in staff meetings, in class, in the services, or driving with them in the car. You will learn so much by being prepared.

Endnotes

1. Maranatha Life, "Life-Line For Pastors"; http://maranathalife.com.

2. "Tsavah"; http://www.studylight.org/lex/heb/view.cgi?number=06680.

3. "Brakah"; http://www.studylight.org/lex/heb/view.cgi?number=01293.

4. *Merriam-Webster's Collegiate Dictionary*, 11th ed., s.v., "Presumption."

CHAPTER EIGHTEEN

TEAM

REMEMBER THAT GOD IS an architect and a builder. God intended us to build and design as He does. God wants us to architecturally design a vision, mission, and team to accomplish His desire. That means that everything we build must be intentional, including picking our team. We must learn to pick our teammates. You will benefit the organization most by becoming an incredible recruiter. Growing organizations need lots of workers; as a leader-servant you will need to be in a constant mode of recruiting and training new workers. True leader-servants don't wait for people to volunteer; they stay attentive to spot possible workers already within the organization. In Acts 6, the disciples were available and simply needed someone to draw out of them what was already inside of them.

Often we spend so much time looking at what we don't have that we look past those who are ready to be trained into what we are looking for. I have always heard that what we need is already in the house. I believe that most of the time this is true. I once heard John Maxwell say with regard to bringing people on your staff and/or team, "If you can't afford to hire the best in the world, hire those who could be the best in the world in the future." What that meant for me was to look in the house for those who have the potential to become the best in the world at what they do. Which meant that I would have to do everything within my power to empower them toward becoming the best in the world.

We cannot be afraid to invest in those who need to be developed. Many leaders prefer to draw from the outside. But I have recognized a difference when a leader both in ministry and in business had the wherewithal to develop from within rather than getting a headhunter or going on a hiring bulletin board to build their team. I am not saying that looking outside is wrong, but I am saying we should also look within. A leader may have to spend more time working on developing the skill of the person that they are raising up, but they will have someone on the team who already has the culture of the organization; in some cases that may make a huge difference over hiring outside skill.

Developing a core member of the team is a long-term commitment, but you may also see fewer turnovers of employees. A young organization who still needs to develop credibility and finances will benefit from looking within. The danger for a young organization will be that what you need in this season may not be the level of skill that you need in the next season. A leader will need to be OK with making necessary changes as the organization grows. The difficulty of this mind-set is that often those who are already in the house are not ready-made. They need you as the leader-servant to develop them into what is needed. If you and I become developers, God will send His best to us *before* they are the best, and we will have the privilege of training them into world-class individuals. There is so much joy in helping someone become what he or she thought he could never become or what she only dreamt of becoming. But it takes looking.

And in those days, the disciples having multiplied, a murmuring of the Hellenists against the Hebrews occurred, because their widows were overlooked in the daily serving.

*And the Twelve called near the multitude of the disciples
and said, It is not pleasing to us, leaving the Word of God,
to serve tables. Therefore, brothers, look out among you seven
men being witnessed to, full of the Holy Spirit and wisdom,
whom we may appoint over this duty* (Acts 6:1-3 MKJV).

Look for people who have the potential to become what the work
needs. Potential is a seed; cultivate that seed and see what grows. God is
a farmer, but He is not a mechanic. Sometimes we want to just place or
replace people as if what we are building is a machine as opposed to a
living organism. Whether it is a ministry, church, school, or business, we
are building with people, which make it organic. It grows and flexes; it
has a soul, and for this reason, we need to cultivate the potential around
us. So take a look around and see who can be developed. When you find
potential, set up some training courses or give them something small to
do so you can evaluate and train them. I have even asked some of these
people with potential for a short-term commitment, like a 60 to 90-day
commitment. All it takes is eyes to see.

Don't look around with doubt and skepticism in your heart, but look
with the faith that God has given you what you need. Maybe you don't see
the person directly in the house; maybe you know someone who is not in
the house, but who is in your life. I have asked people I have met or known
in other settings to join me in the work. Either way, the people that I needed
were in my life already, and I simply talked to them about the vision and
the opportunity. God will touch the hearts of those who are supposed to
help you. Every leader has people who are sent to help in the work. There
may only be one or two in the beginning, but your faithfulness with those
will be the foundation for an army.

*And Samuel said to all the people, Do you see him whom
Jehovah has chosen, that there is none like him among all
the people? And all the people shouted, and said, Let the king*

live! Then Samuel told the people the duties of the kingdom, and wrote in a book and laid it up before Jehovah. And Samuel sent all the people away, each to his house. And Saul also went home to Gibeah. And a band of men went with him, whose hearts God had touched. But the sons of Belial said, How shall this man save us? And they despised him and brought him no present. But he was silent (1 Samuel 10:24-27 MKJV).

Saul's initial group was only a band of men, which later grew into the army of Israel. God is going to touch the hearts of a few who will in turn touch the hearts of others. As you develop your small group, the testimonies of those few will cause others to believe in the work, and their hearts will also be touched. Being faithful and consistent with a few will build credibility, and God will be able to touch the hearts of many to come in the future. One meaning of the word *touch* is "to lay hands upon."[1] God will lay His hands on those whom He desires to be with you. Proverbs 21:1 says, " *The king's heart is in the hand of the Lord, as the rivers of water: He turneth it whithersoever He will*" (KJV). Trust God to move people's hearts to join you and the vision of the house. At the same time, realize that the devil will be moving people's hearts against you.

Sons of Belial

First Samuel 10:27 says that the sons of Belial despised Saul without reason, simply because they didn't believe in Saul. Nor did they believe in God or His prophet. The Bible counsels us to believe God and be established, to believe His prophets and prosper. Samuel had just announced that Saul was the man, and still these men rejected him. Saul didn't ask to be king; actually he hid in the baggage to avoid being seen when his name was mentioned as king. It doesn't have to make sense for people to dislike you and your leaders. The reality is that you can be called, anointed, and appointed, and people will still have an issue with you. Humans usually demand perfection from others, but not from themselves, whatever that standard may be.

The sons of Belial doubted that Saul could save them. It takes faith to see what God is doing. The name Belial tells the whole story. *'Bliya`al bel-e-yah'-al'* means "without profit, worthlessness; destruction, wickedness, evil, naughty, ungodly and wicked."[2] Belial people in the organization will reveal themselves. Their snide remarks and disrespectful statements expose fault-finding attitudes. They'll try to treat you as if you don't have anything more than they do, or as if you don't deserve any uncommon respect—anything to show that they don't recognize your authority. They didn't give Saul a present, nor will they give you a present. You must respond in the same manner as Saul: just stay silent. Take note of those who are with you and those who are not. Never demand respect or try to establish your authority by stating your position. God raised you, and God will defend you. Just make sure that you recognize the Judases or the sons of Belial around you; the last thing you want is to be caught off guard. God will show you who is with you and who is not.

One Sunday morning before service, I went to prayer to prepare for the day. At the time we were planning to move the church. While in prayer I felt prompted by an inward voice that one of the couples on our leadership team would not go with us. When my wife and I got to the church, that couple approached my wife and me to ask for a meeting. We scheduled the meeting, and what I had felt in prayer was confirmed. I have also had people on my team warn me regarding someone that they had a run-in with, or that they feel uncomfortable with. I take these cautions to heart because I believe that God has sent me people on my team who are here to protect my wife and me. We may not do anything about the warning other than simply pay attention, but it helps us make good decisions. My wife really possesses what in 1 Corinthians 12:10 is called *"discerning of spirits."*

In simple terms, the discerning of spirits gives us insight into what is not seen on the surface. She often understands what is happening before the problem arises, which actually gives us time to prepare for the problem if we can't stop the problem.

Your goal for recruiting should be based on a need and desire to commit some aspect of the work over to faithful men and women who have a heart to serve the leaders and vision of the organization.

> *You therefore, my son, be strong in the grace that is in Christ Jesus. And the things that you have heard from me among many witnesses, commit these to faithful men who will be able to teach others also* (2 Timothy 2:1-2).

> *For as we have many members in one body, and all members have not the same office: So we, being many, are one body in Christ, and every one members one of another. Having then gifts differing according to the grace that is given to us, whether prophecy, let us prophesy according to the proportion of faith; or ministry, let us wait on our ministering: or he that teacheth, on teaching; or he that exhorteth, on exhortation: he that giveth, let him do it with simplicity; he that ruleth, with diligence; he that sheweth mercy, with cheerfulness* (Romans 12:4-8 KJV).

A Final Exhortation

Your leadership position affords you grace. Live strong in that grace. People will recognize the strength of the grace and gifts on your life. Know that God has positioned you for such a time as this, for His Kingdom. The first thing in developing your team is to be confident that you are a teacher and a coach. See yourself as a life coach. Posturing yourself as a teacher and a coach will cause a shift in your thinking as well as in the thinking of those you are training. Most people would appreciate a life coach who wants them to become the best that they could be.

Secondly, teach the things that are being taught to you by your leader. If you don't teach them the things that you are learning while sitting at the feet of your leader, then you will end up being the bottleneck that is holding the organization from growing into the vision. Your leader is not looking for you to duplicate yourself and your style and opinions, but for you to take on the vision of the house and duplicate exactly what is in your leaders. The organization can only grow to the level to which the vision and leadership culture has been drilled down in the ranks below you.

Thirdly, *"commit these to faithful men who will be able to teach."* Delegate to faithful men and women who will carry on the teaching. The focus becomes *teach teachers; lead leaders.* This Scripture challenges us to not just find task-oriented people, but to look for teachable people who will not get bogged down in duties. Find people who understand the art and power of duplication. Those new to leadership need to understand that duplication is not an overnight process. It takes commitment and constant adjustments, but if you will pay the price, your efforts will pay high dividends.

Another leader who has made a huge impact on my life is Pastor Kevin Gerald. When I first gave my life to Christ as a young adult, I didn't have any idea of what I was doing. I felt that I was called, but I didn't understand the fullness of that call. Pastor Kevin spent an hour a month with me for a good portion of five years. As someone who grew up without a father and had very few male role models besides my uncles, this was a huge example for me. An hour a month may not seem that much time to invest, but for me, it was worth a lifetime of loyalty. That's how much it changed my life.

You and I have the opportunity to change people's lives with just a little investment of time and coaching. You may have to raise the standard on who to invite to the table after awhile, because the stronger your leadership becomes, the stronger the people who are attracted to your leadership will be. The stronger your leadership becomes, the more challenged your current team will be. Continue to develop everyone that God has touched for your sake with the mind-set that you are going to be able to delegate more and more until they have duplicated you as you have duplicated your own leader. Thoroughly test the faithfulness and capabilities of those who connect with you before you commit the work that your leader has entrusted to you into their hands.

Duplication takes teaching, empowerment, affirmation, and mentoring. Make sure that you have regular, consistent leadership meetings where you teach leadership, life skills, success, and the Word of God in order to keep your team on top of the game. Ensure that your team members have everything they need to get the job done. Empower them with a certain level of authority and the tools necessary to be successful.

Affirm their strengths, and you will notice that they work harder on their weaknesses. Catch them doing something good and celebrate it. Affirm them publicly and in private. Everybody loves to feel good about their work; affirmation makes people feel significant. When people are getting on your nerves, that is the best time to affirm their good qualities.

Mentor and coach any time the opportunity presents itself. Jesus rebuked Peter in Matthew 17:

> *When they came to Capernaum, the collectors of the temple tax came to Peter. They asked him, "Doesn't your teacher pay the temple tax?" "Certainly," he answered. Peter went into the house. Before he could speak, Jesus asked him, "What do you think, Simon? From whom do the kings of the world collect fees or taxes? Is it from their family members or from other people?" "From other people," Peter answered. Jesus said to him, "Then the family members are exempt. However, so that we don't create a scandal, go to the sea and*

*throw in a hook. Take the first fish that you catch. Open its
mouth, and you will find a coin. Give that coin to them for
you and me"* (Matthew 17:24-27 GWD).

Jesus saw an opportunity to coach Peter into another level of integrity and responsibility by asking Peter about his tax problem. Don't put off any opportunities to teach your team. When you see something wrong and you have a moment to use it as a chance to teach, then take that open door immediately. After Peter learned his lesson, Jesus empowered him and gave Peter a second chance to make the right decision. As a coach, it is necessary to allow people an opportunity to change once they have seen their wrong.

Mentoring involves coaching, modeling, evaluation, retooling, and correction. You must invest in the lives of the people you lead. Remember that they will do the same for the leader-servants whom they lead. Don't be afraid to evaluate and correct those whom you lead; they and the organization will be better off. The Bible advises us in Ephesians 4:15 to speak the *"truth in love,* [that we] *may grow up into Him in all things, which is the head—Christ."* Mentoring demands that you speak the truth in love. Just because you tell the truth doesn't mean that it is told in love. Your attitude speaks much, much louder than your words. The foundation of mentoring, be it coaching, modeling, evaluation, or correction, must be love. The motivation is to make the person who receives the instruction a better person and leader, not so that you can correct and feel better about it yourself. You never need to be harsh to mentor or to correct. Look how Jesus did it with Peter—He asked him probing and thought-provoking questions, which led Peter to another level of understanding. Then Peter was teachable and ready to carry out the instructions of his leader. Mentoring is a vital part of building a world-class team.

Build a team that will build the organization. Build an organization that builds the Kingdom of God. Live a full and strong life in the grace of

God for you and your leader. Grow every single day. Be a lifetime learner. Celebrate every day. Laugh out loud every day. Obey God with all of your heart every day. Commune with the Holy Spirit first thing every day. Exercise, eat healthy, and think healthy. Be a family man or woman. Let people love you. Be a teachable, positive leader whom your leader can lean on. Be the coach on the field. Be an obedient follower. Be a loyal leader-servant. May God bless you in everything your hand touches and your feet tread upon!

Endnotes

1. *Merriam-Webster's Collegiate Dictionary*, 11ᵗʰ ed., s.v., "Touch."

2. "Belial"; http://www.studylight.org/lex/heb/view.cgi?number=01100.

TRACEY ARMSTRONG

P.O Box 78096
Seattle, WA 98178
Telephone: 206-722-5757

Church: Citadel Church
www.citadelchurch.com

Ministry: Lionheart Ministries
www.lionheartministries.com

www.traceyarmstrong.com

www.followership.me